MODERN WORLD NATIONS

Canada

Kristi L. Desaulniers

Series Consulting Editor
Charles F. Gritzner
South Dakota State University

CHELSEA HOUSE
PUBLISHERS
A Haights Cross Communications Company

hiladelphia

Frontispiece: Flag of Canada

Cover: Bow Lake, Banff National Park, Alberta.

CHELSEA HOUSE PUBLISHERS

VP, NEW PRODUCT DEVELOPMENT Sally Cheney
DIRECTOR OF PRODUCTION Kim Shinners
CREATIVE MANAGER Takeshi Takahashi
MANUFACTURING MANAGER Diann Grasse

Staff for CANADA

EDITOR Lee Marcott
PRODUCTION EDITOR Jaimie Winkler
PICTURE RESEARCHER 21st Century Publishing and Communications, Inc.
COVER DESIGNER Keith Trego, SERIES DESIGNER Takeshi Takahashi
LAYOUT 21st Century Publishing and Communications, Inc.

A Haights Cross Communications Company

http://www.chelseahouse.com

First Printing

1 3 5 7 9 8 6 4 2

Library of Congress Cataloging-in-Publication Data

Desaulniers, Kristi L.
    Canada / Kristi L. Desaulniers.
        p. cm.—(Modern world nations)
Includes index.
Contents: Introducing Canada—Physical landscapes—Canada through time—Faces and places—Government—Economy—Living in Canada today—Canada looks ahead.
    ISBN 0-7910-7238-X HC   0-7910-7501-X PB
    1. Canada—Juvenile literature. [1. Canada.] I. Title. II. Series.
F1008.2 .D45 2002
971—dc21

2002015799

Table of Contents

Canada

Moraine Lake in British Columbia sparkles at the base of rocky, pine-scrub mountains, illustrating the variety of dramatic natural resources Canada offers. Vacationers and other tourists appreciate the mountains for their cold-weather sports during winter; in warm weather, the higher elevations offer relief from the summertime heat.

Introducing Canada

I magine you are hiking on a meandering trail through one of Canada's spectacular national parks. As you breathe in deeply, smelling the natural perfume of the evergreens surrounding you in this particular location, you pause to wonder, "Have I experienced Canada before?"

If you have eaten a crisp, juicy McIntosh apple (cultivated in Ontario in 1811 by John McIntosh), you have experienced a taste of Canada! As you zip your backpack, thank Canada for this modern, gripping innovation. Telephones, utilizing technology developed by Canadian resident Alexander Graham Bell in 1876, are an innovation we all have used. The snowmobile, insulin usage for diabetics, and the use of wood pulp for newsprint are other prominent Canadian innovations depended on throughout the world. In fact, 40 percent of the world's newspapers are printed on newsprint manufactured from Canada's lumber industry.

With a land area of 3.8 million square miles (nearly 10 million square kilometers), Canada is the world's second-largest country. It also dominates the northern portion of the North American continent. Three oceans—the Pacific, Arctic, and Atlantic—border Canada's shores. An undefended land border of 5,524 miles, the longest in the world, is shared with the continental United States to the south and with the state of Alaska to the northwest. Because of Canada's tremendous size, the mountains merge with the gently rolling hills of the interior plains and the arctic tundra with ease. Canada's vibrant cities and liberal history for welcoming immigrants make this country a desirable home for some 31 million people. This population, however, when considered with the vast land area, gives Canada one of the world's lowest population densities—about 8 people per square mile.

Marked regional differences are visible in Canada's physical and human landscapes. The diversity of Canada's physical environment ranges from the quiet coves and beaches of the Atlantic Provinces to the fertile grasslands of central Canada's prairies. Numerous lakes dot the rocky cradle of the Canadian Shield, where animals greatly outnumber the people (and mosquitoes outnumber animals!). It is in this core of the North American continent where Hudson's Bay Company thrived as a result of its fur trade. "The Bay," which once owned over 10 percent of the entire earth's surface, is still in business as the world's oldest company.

Diverse peoples sprinkled throughout the varied landscapes offer seasoning for Canada's colorful heritage and history. Populated historically with aboriginal (native) populations, early cultures were able to take advantage of Canada's blessing of abundant natural elements. Fish, whales, buffalo, and other forms of wildlife were life-sustaining resources. Numerous water routes eased travel and provided access to the interior of the country and additional resources. The richness of the country's resource base also attracted European explorers and settlers who began arriving, with an inquisitive purpose, nearly five centuries ago. This mysterious land offered potential to fulfill a quest for the Northwest Passage, a desired route sought between Europe and the rich markets of the "Orient." Centuries-long pursuits would bring extended contacts with aboriginal peoples already populating Canada.

Reliance on aboriginal knowledge was beneficial for these explorations. Maps were sketched from memory on birch bark, in the snow, and on the ground by the aboriginal peoples. This wealth of knowledge was often incorporated onto maps drawn by early European explorers.

It was during one of these European meetings with Iroquoian peoples that the name of Canada was first applied. French explorer Jacques Cartier inquired about the land he was exploring in 1535 near present-day Québec City. The Iroquoian response was "kanata," the Huron-Iroquois word for "village" or "settlement." Maps in 1547 thus began showing reference to land north of the St. Lawrence River as "Canada."

What has molded a unique Canadian identity? From ancient human activity in the Yukon Territory to complexities in government and economy, you will get a glimpse of the defining identities of Canada as you read this book. The faces and places that greet you with impressive diversity offer an invitation to explore.

In our minds, we all possess "mental maps" of our *location*, or where we live. These maps aid us in defining *place*, or what it is like there. Picture where you are right now in relation to your home or school. What landmarks do you pass on the way there? Why is that landmark located where it is? What foods are available, or not available, in your community? Why? How are people dressed? What forms of transportation do you use to get around and what routes to you prefer to take? Your mental map is built of experiences and what you have learned about a particular location.

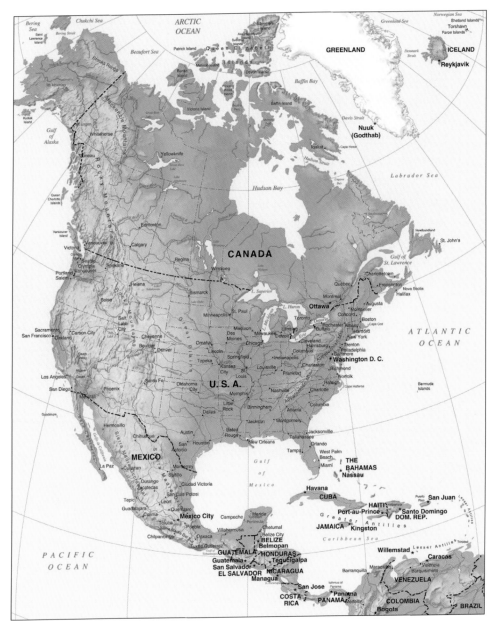

Canada's land area alone is almost 4 million square miles (nearly 10 million square kilometers). The U.S.–Canadian border stretches for 5,524 miles, and some southern portions of Canada dip below the more northerly U.S. cities. Canada's three other borders are bounded by oceans, holding within them land that varies from ice-topped mountains to fertile farmland.

You are also developing mental maps about the country in which you live. You know the significant holidays celebrated there and the favorite destinations your family likes to visit for fun and relaxation. Learning about Canada by reading books such as this one also helps to create the images you carry in your mind about this country. Asking the questions "Why?" or "Why should we care?" will add more color and impact to the mental maps, impressions, and pictures you are developing. Geographers ask these questions as they study and observe their surroundings. You can, too!

Consider your mental map of Canada. What comes to mind? Perhaps jagged mountain ridges, the hollow song of a loon, prairie grasslands, chocolate-brown moose sloshing through marshy lakes, or creeping ice-blue glaciers. Your mental map of Canada may also include the Toronto Blue Jays, beckoning lighthouses, or sweet drops of golden maple syrup! As you read about Canada, your mental map will be sharpened, and details will become clear. Questions will come to mind. The delight of a journey through such a beautiful country as Canada may lead you to this fascinating land. What is Canada like? Let the experiences of reading and asking geographic questions begin to show you the answers.

Immigrants—who utilized the transcontinental railroad to reach central and western lands—established many of Canada's lush farms. Even though the number of farms in Canada is decreasing, the size and productivity of individual farms remain strong and are even increasing. As more industry moves into Canada, the farmers also take advantage of new technology to keep up with consumer needs and trends.

Canadian Shield

West of the Atlantic Maritimes is the rocky, lake-dotted physical landscape of the Canadian Shield. This unique geologic region is considered by scientists to be the core of the North American continent. Also known as the Laurentian Plateau, the Canadian Shield is composed of the continent's most ancient surface rock, formed billions of years ago. It covers more than one-half the country's land area and is responsible for the physical separation of eastern from western Canada. Hudson Bay lies in the heart of the Shield. During the Ice Age, when the area was covered by thousands of feet of glacial ice, a huge indentation was created on Earth's surface by the tremendous weight of the glacial ice mass. The Hudson Bay now occupies this basin. When the ice retreated, the land began to rebound—a process still underway. It is this rebound, or land rising, that has created the steep coastal cliffs along part of Hudson Bay (and much of the north shore of Lake Superior).

The Shield is a region of vast resource wealth. It is a storehouse of minerals, including iron and nickel. It also has huge waterpower potential and is home to one of the world's largest unbroken expanses of forest. In addition, the solitude of its lakes, rivers, and varied wildlife is a greatly appreciated ecological resource. Scraped by the advance and retreat of glacial activity, gouges left in the rock collected water in their basins and crevices. This ancient Precambrian (Shield) rock is strewn with countless bogs, swamps, ponds, lakes, and rivers. With so much water occupying the surface, transportation linkages are costly to build and are therefore few in number. Most travel here must be by air, testing the skills of Canada's famous "bush pilots" and their sturdy workhorse planes—equipped with pontoons for summer, and skis for winter. Because the soil here is shallow and poor in quality—and surface transportation so difficult—this region supports a very low population.

The Great Lakes–St. Lawrence Lowlands

This region of Canada extends across a narrow belt of southern Ontario and Québec along the Canadian–U.S. border. This relatively small area has many towns and cities, including Toronto, Ottawa, Montréal, and Québec City. Much of the region is the most southerly in Canada, near Canada's border with the United States. People living here—nearly one-half of all Canadians—actually live south, in terms of latitude, of the U.S. boundary between Washington and Oregon. Milder temperatures, abundant level land, rich soils, and ease of transportation on the St. Lawrence River initially attracted people to live in this narrow belt. The luxurious agricultural land that once attracted many settlers to this region is still utilized for farming, but large areas of farmland are being slowly transformed into urban and industrial use, and therefore are being lost to agricultural production.

The five Great Lakes form a connected system that is the world's largest body of fresh water. They are linked to the Atlantic Ocean by the largest river in eastern Canada, the St. Lawrence. The moderating (warming) effects of lakes Erie and Ontario extend the frost-free days of the Niagara Peninsula, allowing peaches, grapes, and pears to grow extensively. Additionally, the waterways of the Great Lakes and the St. Lawrence River remain ice-free for much of the year, thus offering this inland region access to the Atlantic Ocean and to other places of the world through a linking system of rivers and canals. A visible physical boundary, the ridge of the Niagara Escarpment, begins to separate the agricultural lowlands from the forested Canadian Shield to the north.

Interior Plains

The Interior Plains form an immense region of nearly level grassland bordered by the Canadian Shield to the east and the Canadian Rockies to the west. Ancient Lake Agassiz, formed

These sandstone formations are called "hoodoos." Visit the Red Deer River Valley of southern Alberta, and you'll see these pillars, created by the erosive effects of wind and water. Erosion in this area also yielded an archaeological surprise: dinosaur fossils.

nearly 12,000 years ago from glacial meltwater, once covered much of the southern Interior Plains, especially Manitoba and Saskatchewan. After "drying up" approximately 7,000 years ago (the largest body of water remaining from Lake Agassiz is present-day Lake Winnipeg), a rich layer of soil was left behind on the former lake bed. This soil forms the basis for much of central Canada's agricultural wealth. Rich grain-producing regions in Alberta and Saskatchewan, of wheat especially, make Canada one of the world's major exporters of grain. Surprisingly, the waving fields of golden wheat so familiar to the landscape today were introduced by farmers only in the last century.

The strange-looking sandstone "hoodoos" of southern Alberta are another surprise in the region's natural landscape.

These spirit-like pillars, created by the erosive effects of wind and water, are located in the Red Deer River Valley. Erosion also has exposed layers of rock and dinosaur fossils, uncovering rich concentrations of dinosaur remains. The Athabasca Oil Sands in Alberta have been of use since First Nations (the preferred term for groups popularly referred to, although incorrectly, as "Indians") used the material to waterproof canoes in the late 1700s.

The Cordillera

The Spanish origin of the word *cordillera* means "parallel ridges." Starting from the Canadian Rockies and extending west to the Pacific Ocean, this region offers spectacular vertically oriented scenery that contrasts physically with the flatter, horizontal beauty of the Interior Plains. The young mountain ranges here, including the Coastal and St. Elias Mountains, run in parallel ridges from the northern borders on the Beaufort Sea along the western coast, southward into western Mexico. Where the mountains meet the sea, many deep and narrow inlets called *fjords* are formed. Ice Age glaciers scoured these scenic, steep-sided arms of the sea. As is true throughout the Pacific Rim region, earthquakes pose a constant threat to land, property, and life in western Canada. High plateaus and deep valleys offer further variety in the physical landscape. Additionally, the lush, rain-nourished forests and the gardens of coastal British Columbia near Vancouver and Victoria receive the benefits of a coastal Pacific location. Yet, on the leeward (the side sheltered from the wind; here, eastern) side of the mountains, a rain-shadow effect forces Okanogan Valley farmers to irrigate orchards and vineyards. Because the wind cannot blow "through" the mountain, this protected area remains dry when rain blows in and falls on the windward (unprotected) side of the mountain. Here, cactus can even be found growing in some protected areas.

These running ridges of parallel mountain ranges posed engineering difficulties for the development of the transcontinental railways and highways. The majority of the region's population is contained in the more accessible southwestern part of British Columbia, linked to the Pacific Ocean in the dense population clusters of Vancouver and Victoria. This is true as well in the population clusters of Yukon Territory where southwestern access to the Pacific Ocean is available.

The Arctic North

This region is often described as located north of the 60th parallel of latitude. Consisting of the Yukon, Northwest Territories, and Nunavut, the Arctic North comprises approximately 40 percent of Canada's land area. The region "overlaps" the Canadian Shield to both the north and east. Straits and sounds (inlets) separate the maze of islands in the Arctic North and link to form the elusive Northwest Passage, a waterway route sought by several early explorers.

Just beyond the tree line of the boreal forest, the Arctic North has a treeless region known as the *tundra*. It is a cold, barren, windswept, and seemingly forbidding region; yet for several thousand years, it has been home to the Inuit (Eskimo) people. The *permafrost* layer of its soil is frozen year-round; the shallow covering of surface soil above the permafrost thaws during the summer months, when daylight is nearly continuous. Even though the frost-free season is brief, its almost-constant sunlight coaxes small delicate flowers, lichens, and mosses to life, carpeting the surface. The ground often becomes swampy during this time of year—much of the land is so flat that drainage is poor. The snow that does thaw cannot seep into the frozen ground, so it remains on the surface. The resulting bogs of spongy surface soil are called "muskeg." All too soon, the long, dark, bitterly cold winters return to the tundra, and the surface soil freezes hard again.

Meanwhile, even farther north, the polar ice cap remains frozen year-round.

WEATHER AND CLIMATE

Weather describes present atmospheric conditions, whereas *climate* describes the long-term averages of weather patterns. Canada's diverse weather and climate—and their resulting effects—are evident in its variety of landscapes, which range from lush, moisture-fed rain forests to windswept treeless tundra; polar deserts to sun-nourished grain fields; luscious peach orchards to salty windstorms.

Canada's weather and climate are influenced by a combination of factors. They include latitude, elevation, slope, pressure and wind patterns, water features, and the orientation of major landform features. For instance, in the low-lying area of White River, Ontario, cool evening air settles and drains downslope, creating a "frost hollow" more than 300 days per year on average.

Because of Canada's northerly latitude, the sun's rays strike the earth's surface at a low angle, resulting in winters that are long and cold, and summers that are short and warm (but not hot). Elevation has a large influence on Canada's climate and weather as well; for example, the amount and frequency of precipitation at higher elevations is greater on the windward (unprotected) side of a mountain range. This is evident in the Cordillera region of Canada, where the mountain ranges also act as barriers to prevent moisture-laden Pacific air from entering Canada's interior. While the air mass does move over these ranges, most of its moisture is evaporated by the time the air reaches Alberta. Also, temperatures decrease with increased elevation, resulting in cooler weather in the mountains—and attractive summer vacation spots. It also explains why many mountain peaks are covered with snow (or glacier) all year.

The open flatness of the Canadian prairies makes the area

Mount Tupper in Glacier National Park is a picture-perfect snow-covered peak. Because of the high elevations in the Canadian Rockies, the air at the top of the mountains stays cooler, and some craggy summits are covered with snow year-round.

susceptible to invading Arctic cold winds in the winter and hot, dry southerly winds in the summer. Yet, the Chinook winds (dry, warm winds due to air compression as they descend the eastern slope of the Rocky Mountains) can change this susceptibility in a short time.

As you may recall, central Canada is dominated by the saucer-shaped Canadian Shield with Hudson Bay in the Shield's core. Despite the ruggedness of the bogs, lakes, and rocky outcroppings, air stream movement is affected very minimally by the Shield's overall landscape.

Larger bodies of water such as the Great Lakes have a profound influence on climate. Water heats up more slowly than land and holds the heat longer once it is absorbed. As a result, these large bodies of water have a moderating effect on the climate of southern and eastern Canada, keeping those regions slightly warmer than they otherwise might be.

The Pacific Coastal region is generally warm and moist. Prevailing westerly winds blow across the warm waters of the Pacific, carrying both moisture and warmth over land. The Atlantic Provinces, however, receive prevailing westerly winds from the continent's interior. When winds do arrive onshore from the east, they have traveled across the icy waters of the Labrador Current. This current flows from the arctic region and brings cool temperatures and high humidity—conditions that combine to create bone-chilling weather.

The Arctic Ocean of Canada's northern polar region, with its drifting ice and enormous fields of pack ice, offers little help moderating the cold. However, heat conducted through the ice does keep winter temperatures from reaching the extremes that often occur over land. During the "warmer" months from June through August, ice fog and Arctic "sea smoke" form over breaks in the ice pack.

Temperature ranges vary greatly from one location to another. The average *annual temperature range* is figured by subtracting the average temperature of the coldest month from the average temperature of the warmest month. For example, the annual temperature range difference in the central Northwest Territories is 104°F (58°C), compared to a 50°F (28°C) annual temperature range along the Pacific Coast. Typical annual temperature ranges are 95°F (53°C) for the

Prairie Provinces, 86°F (48°C) for the Great Lakes–St. Lawrence Seaway region, and 73°F (41°C) for the Atlantic Maritimes. (Remember that these are temperature *ranges*, not temperature averages.)

Precipitation (moisture that reaches the ground as rain, hail, sleet, or snow) is heaviest along Canada's Pacific Coast in British Columbia. Here, the annual precipitation levels can exceed 90 inches (229 centimeters), while in southeastern Alberta the levels rarely exceed 15 inches (38 centimeters). The country's precipitation is unevenly distributed in both geographic location and time, as is shown by the arid conditions of the rain-shadowed regions, polar deserts, and the desert oasis near Osoyoos, in British Columbia near the border with central Washington.

Along with the precipitation and sunshine Canada receives, the country also is ventilated by winds of varying strength, temperature, and humidity. Tales of early peoples are filled with many and varied images of local winds. Some names refer to the origin or destination of the wind, some describe the coldness or warmth of the air, while others are descriptive of either pleasant or trying times. One image defines a "barber" as a strong wind bringing precipitation that freezes to your hair upon contact! Additionally, Canada experiences thunderstorms, tornadoes, blizzards, and occasional hurricanes. So perhaps it is more appropriate to speak of the *climates* of such an immense country as Canada.

VEGETATION AND ANIMAL LIFE

If asked to name one tree species found in Canada, what would your response be? Sugar Maple? Spruce? Tulipwood? Alder? You would be correct if you named any one of these trees. For logging and paper pulp, there are the boreal (evergreen) forests of the mid-north. Sugar maples, found mainly in southeastern Canada, are a significant resource for beautiful furniture, maple syrup, and fiery-colored leafscapes in the autumn.

Canada's many waterways–lakes, rivers, and streams–and their surrounding vegetative areas are home to a diverse assortment of animal life. Canada is known for such land mammals as moose, deer, and mink. In addition, beavers, loons, and the ever-present Canada goose thrive throughout many regions.

The mixed prairie (tall and short grass) vegetation of the Interior Plains contrasts with the boreal forests of the cooler, moister conditions of the mid-north. Near the polar ice cap, there is little or no vegetation to soften the horizon.

Living among these vegetative areas are many land mammals such as moose, deer, and mink. The lakes, rivers, and streams offer a comfortable habitat for the slippery beavers, singing loons, and Canadian Geese. Polar bears, caribou with snowshoe-like hooves, and ptarmigan (grouse) feel right at home in their Arctic environment! As for the puffin, harp seals, beluga whales, and salmon, they are plentiful in their northern aquatic habitats.

WATER FEATURES AND SOILS

The Grand Banks, a continental shelf lying beneath shallow water off coastal Newfoundland, have been called the "wheat fields" of Newfoundland because of the resource potential. Cool, northern waters from Labrador mix with warmer currents from the south, resulting in one of the world's richest fishing grounds. Yet even their enormous fish populations have proven to be vulnerable. Severe overfishing has resulted in a sharp decrease in the supply of fish in recent years. Newfoundlanders have a renewed interest in the area below the waters, however, as oil has recently been discovered there.

Since the earliest period of European settlement, the St. Lawrence River has been a vital link joining Canadians to the global sea. The river also is an important source of hydroelectric power (electricity produced with the assistance of moving water) for Canada's increasing population. The hydropower of Niagara Falls, harnessed in the past century, likewise provides energy for homes and factories in addition to energizing the tourism industry. Streams and rivers flowing into Hudson Bay can also be added to the list of hydroelectric producers.

The Fraser River in British Columbia is significant as a life-line for the run of various salmon species. Its estuary is home for many varieties of aquatic birds, and raptor migrations also define the importance of the Fraser River. No matter where they are located, Canada's water resources—rivers, lakes, bays, and oceans—offer sustaining qualities for humans and many other living things.

Canada's Prairie Provinces, as well as basin and river valleys in both the southwest and southeast, contain generally fertile soils. Perhaps one of the most striking soils is the red earth found on Prince Edward Island. The red coloring is due to the presence of iron oxide that "rusts" upon exposure to air.

MINERAL RESOURCES

Forty percent of Canada's minerals are located in the Canadian Shield. Nickel, iron, uranium, silver, zinc, cobalt, copper, and gold are mined here. Because of the difficulty of access, many deposits remain unexploited; in fact, it is believed that many deposits may not yet have been discovered. Some of these minerals are also found in the territories of the Arctic North. Additionally, nonrenewable resources such as oil and natural gas are prevalent in the western Prairie Provinces and also in the North.

Yukon, meaning "greatest" in the native vocabulary, more properly describes the mineral resources that remain mostly unearthed in this territory. The discovery of gold in the Yukon touched off the famed Klondike Gold Rush of 1897, opening up another frontier to increased settlement. A recently opened diamond mine in the Northwest Territories will eventually contribute perhaps 5 percent of the world's supply of this gemstone. Coal, silica (used in making windows and other glass objects), and manganese offer a sampling of other mineral resources being excavated from the earth's crust in Canada.

ENVIRONMENTAL CONCERNS

The condition of the physical environment has emerged as a key concern throughout the world. Realizing their dependence on the environment and its natural resources, Canadians are working to address their environmental concerns. A recent enactment of a revised Canadian Environmental Protection Act focuses on reducing and preventing pollution that results from energy acquisition and energy usage. Renewable energy sources such as hydro-electricity and wind power are gaining increased attention. Flooding of important ecological zones resulting from the building of dams, as well as the accelerating loss of agricultural lands to urban sprawl, remain a concern of Canada's environmental well-being. Canadians are working to protect the environment for present and future generations.

Canada's First Nations, far from being primitive, were quite knowledgeable about their surroundings. They hunted, gathered, fished, and farmed to sustain themselves on the land. Where possible, they lived settled lifestyles; elsewhere, they traveled according to the seasons and available food.

Canada Through Time

T he self-governing Dominion of Canada—comprised of Ontario, Québec, New Brunswick, and Nova Scotia—was established on July 1, 1867. But is this date the real beginning of Canada as a country? At this point in the young country's life, Canada still maintained ties to the British crown. (This unique connection will be further discussed in Chapter 5, when you will read about Canada's government.)

The date that dominion status was achieved makes Canada a young country—less than two centuries old. But Canada has an extensive history leading up to July 1, 1867, one that weaves human existence into Canada's fabric thousands of years earlier. Early human activity is proven with evidence from the Yukon Territory's

Bluefish Caves. Here, archaeologists have dated woolly mammoth bones, patterned with fractures indicative of butchering, at approximately 25,000 years old. To understand Canada today, we must begin thousands of years ago, then work through the country's tangled history to the present time.

THE BERING LAND BRIDGE AND THE ICE-FREE CORRIDOR

Glacial sheets of ice once covered nearly all of Canada, with the exception of portions of the Yukon. These ice sheets ranged in thickness from several hundred yards to more than two miles! This glaciation of the Last Ice Age (Pleistocene Era) occurred until approximately 10,000 years ago. Because a huge volume of ocean water fell as snow over land and became frozen into glaciers, the level of the Bering Sea dropped to a level that exposed portions of continental shelves. The exposed shelves created a wide land "bridge" joining what is now eastern Siberia with the state of Alaska.

Similarities exist in burins (chisel-like tools) and microblades (sharp-edged flakes of stone embedded in bone) of both the Siberian peoples and the First Peoples of the unglaciated territory of the Yukon. This link offers support for the Bering Land Bridge theory—the belief that the first Americans arrived from Asia, by land. These linked tools were necessary items for processing woolly mammoths after a hunt. Mammoths offered survival for these early people in a harsh, cold environment. Much of what is known about this period of time comes from archaeological research of human artifacts and remains. By researching tools and other remains of inhabited locations, ways of life begin to unfold. As the woolly mammoth population moved, so did these early Native ancestors.

Changes occurred as glaciers began to retreat (melt). Water levels rose and the Bering Land Bridge became submerged. The climate of North America began to warm, bringing further adaptations to cultural patterns—skills, knowledge, and behaviors. As the woolly mammoth died off, these early humans adapted to changing environmental conditions. They began to hunt other large game and, eventually, whales and seals.

Some scientists doubt the theory of early migrations by way of an ice-free corridor. They believe that conditions on land were too cold and harsh; in fact, some doubt whether an ice-free route ever even existed between the towering glaciers that covered the region. They offer another theory to explain how the first humans could have reached the Americas: that early peoples could have traveled along an open and much warmer water route, following the coast from Asia to North America. There is some evidence provided by artifacts discovered along the Pacific shores of Canada and the United States that offers at least some support for this idea.

While the migratory route continues to be of scientific interest, it is of little importance to us. We know that Canada was settled tens of thousands of years ago. The earliest evidence of human presence in what is now Canada traces back only some 25,000 years. But some archaeologists believe that it may have been earlier, perhaps as long as 40,000 years ago.

ABORIGINAL PEOPLES

When eventual European exploration occurred, Canada was already populated by diverse groups of native people. Each geographic region presented its own set of environmental conditions to which early settlers adapted their lifestyles. The Native People were hunters, gatherers, fishers, and, later, farmers. Some lived settled lifestyles while others were nomadic, moving with the seasons and food sources. Although some people might incorrectly think of them as having been "primitive," they had to possess a powerful knowledge of the land and its resources in order to survive.

Of special note were the Huron. They lived along the

southeastern corner of the Great Lake that now bears their name—Lake Huron. This location was a north–south trade crossroads. Here, linkages and networks of aboriginal North America crisscrossed. The Huron also dominated interior trade routes east to the Atlantic Ocean. An Iroquois-speaking population had a presence in the woodlands of this area as well. As European settlements spread westerly from the Atlantic Coast, native ways of life for all native peoples would be affected.

THULE CULTURE: 9TH AND 10TH CENTURIES

Inuit peoples (Eskimos) arrived in northern Canada perhaps 6,000 years ago. Approximately 1,000 years ago, a climatic warming occurred throughout the Arctic. The Thule, a whale-hunting people, took advantage of this development, traveling by *umiak* (a boat with a skin-covered frame and several seats for passengers and supplies) through partially thawed waters. Migrating whalers were equipped with sophisticated sea-hunting tools and techniques. Included were such items as detachable-head harpoons and multiple groupings of inflated sealskins used to slow harpooned whales. To the east and north, in Baffin Bay, waters were open and whale populations of the time were plentiful, encouraging exploration and the search for additional resources.

Thule villages were located along northern coastal areas of Arctic Canada. Other natural resources, such as seal and caribou, sustained the Thule where whales were not plentiful or available; near Igloolik, on a small island west of Baffin Island, walrus offered a diversified hunting option. The Thule used bones from these animals as building materials, and their skins as roofs—creating what must have been a warm, smoky atmosphere in efficient dwellings. Within a period of a few hundred years, the Thule culture had spread throughout Arctic Canada. Subsequent climatic cooling, which began around 1200 A.D., may have begun the decline of the

Champlain had hopes for converting the Native populations from their traditional ways to the ways of Roman Catholicism. Champlain hoped that passing on the strong Catholic influence would be accomplished by missionary work with the Native People. However, the Native People already had their own strong beliefs and did not always welcome the efforts of the missionaries. As a third effort, Champlain wanted to further develop fur trade with the native populations.

The expanse of Champlain's dream of a fur-trading empire would come true beyond his imagination! French explorers, trappers, and traders journeyed west across the Canadian prairies, paddled north to Hudson Bay, and ventured south to the Gulf of Mexico. The legacy of these French trappers continues today in the hundreds of French place names that dot the linguistic landscape across much of the United States and Canada.

The success of Champlain's efforts depended greatly on establishing positive relationships with native peoples already living there. Champlain did this by exploring much of the provinces known today as Québec and Ontario on foot and by canoe. Often, native guides, sharing their impressive knowledge of the land, accompanied him. Strong trading partnerships were formed with natives. The Huron, a powerful nation of hunters, farmers, and traders, were included in these ties.

Not to be forgotten, the British were sending Henry Hudson across the Atlantic Ocean. He located a bay that is named for him, Hudson Bay, in 1610. The European powers of France and Britain were both coveting the domination of global trade. Both empires treasured "newly discovered" lands. France claimed central Canada, including much of present-day Ontario. The British, in Hudson Bay, also lay claim to much of the same land. It was inevitable that, in time, the conflicts of these interests would escalate.

NEW FRANCE: 17TH CENTURY

Harsh landscapes and challenging climates made life difficult for people who settled in New France in the early years. Few people wanted to move there from France because of the hardships. In fact, the population of New France by the 1660s—after a half-century of occupation—was estimated to be only about 3,000 people.

Samuel de Champlain and those Europeans who arrived soon after confirmed the importance of settling along the St. Lawrence River Valley. The lake and river systems made westward exploration comfortable for thousands of miles—the rough Appalachian terrain to the east was daunting to early explorers. Additionally, the country was rich with fur for trade—risky, but it did sustain New France for many years. The concentrated search for furs also took the French into the Great Lakes region and south along the Mississippi River into land that would later become part of the United States.

Jesuit missionaries sought to convert the Huron and other native populations to Roman Catholicism, the religion of the French, just as Champlain had hoped. The French believed that by establishing Roman Catholicism among the native populations their relationships with the Huron and their trading partners would be unified and further strengthened. Establishing peace among the native nations themselves was also an important endeavor pursued by the missionaries. The Huron homelands were the hub of the inland fur trade; however, the Iroquois sought to take control of this lucrative trade. As French relations with the Huron tightened, the Iroquois became increasingly hostile toward both parties. Rivalries escalated in tribal trading as well as in European trading.

RIVALRY BETWEEN BRITISH AND FRENCH

British settlers had hoped to establish themselves on the northern fringes of New France. In the 1660s, they received help from two French traders, Sieur des Groseilliers and Pierre-Esprit Radisson. Upset by the high costs of transporting furs to Québec and the heavy tax on furs, these two became "traitors" when they fled to New England (a developing British colonial region in the northeastern United States), then gradually made their way to England to rally support from London merchants. They urged Britain to provide support to establish fur trading posts in the Hudson Bay area. Upon seeing a shipload of furs from the region, the King of England agreed. His approval led to the formation of the Hudson's Bay Company in 1670. The Company assumed power over all land in the Hudson Bay drainage basin—well over 1,000,000 square miles (2,590,000 square kilometers) of land representing approximately one-third of present-day Canada. The land became known as Rupert's Land, named after the head of the Hudson's Bay Company.

Now, with fur traders on the bay, fisherman on the Atlantic Coast, and explorers still searching for the Northwest Passage, the British were nosing around the north and south of New France. Caught between the Iroquois to the south and the Hudson's Bay Company to the north, New France pushed into the interior. Since the sixteenth century, France and England had been competing to develop colonies in this New World. It would not be long until the competition led to intensified conflict and war.

THE WAR YEARS: 1754 THROUGH 1763

In 1749, the governor of New France declared an advance into the Ohio River Valley, land that had not yet been claimed by New France. Its possession would confine British colonists and their fur trade to the area east of the Allegheny Mountains. Almost immediately, this threatened the British colonies' expansion, fur trade, and opportunities for settlement. By 1753, feelings of dissent escalated to action. A British colonists' expedition, under the leadership of George

Washington, traveled to the forks of the Ohio River.

Known in America as the French and Indian War, the European-named Seven Years' War began in approximately 1754. The two sides seemed unbalanced at first, with British colonists numbering nearly 1,000,000 compared to 70,000 for New France. But several thousand Indian allies supported the French. This, in combination with more organized and better-trained French troops, led to early French victories. It also offered a showcase for the strength and resolve of the yearning-to-be-independent, future country of Canada. Nonetheless, in 1758, the British captured the thick-walled and heavily cannoned French fortress of Louisbourg on Cape Breton Island. In 1759, the British had another victory on the Plains of Abraham (named after the farmer who owned the land) in Québec City. This famous battle ended French rule in Canada, and Québec City fell to the British. The Treaty of Paris in 1763 officially surrendered French territory east of the Mississippi River to Great Britain.

BRITISH NORTH AMERICA: 1763 THROUGH THE EARLY 1800s

The British victory reduced the threat from New France to the developing "American" colonies, thus lessening those colonies' dependence on Great Britain. The victory also allowed for continuation of the fur trade. Additionally, it presented the colonies with a large population of French-speaking inhabitants in Québec. Under British rule, Parliament proclaimed the Québec Act of 1774, which essentially extended the boundaries of New France to the south and west. Thus, New France was now under British North American rule. The Act also recognized the in-place *seigneurial* system. Under this system, farmers rented land from a landlord (called a *seigneur*), rather than owning it. At this time, Canada retained the Roman Catholic Church and did not enforce the prominent Protestant religion of the British. Thus, the British permitted French

Although Britain defeated France in the Seven Years' War, the British allowed French traditions to remain, including the retention of the Roman Catholic Church. The new British North American colonies still had a large number of French-speaking residents in Québec, setting the stage for talk of Québec's secession two centuries later.

traditions, and people were allowed to remain where they had settled. (To this day, a struggle continues over issues of Québec's desire to be a sovereign, independent nation.)

The American Revolution (War of Independence) in 1776 also had a profound impact on Canada. Many colonists in the 13 U.S. colonies wanted to sever ties with England, but those who wished to remain associated with England were threatened with loss of homes, jobs, and even their lives. Many moved north to seek refuge in Canada. Because of their loyalty to the British Empire, they were called "United Empire Loyalists." Nearly 40,000 Loyalists were welcomed in Canada. These ties to England would be influential to Canada's future political system and government.

The large influx of populations led to the creation of Upper Canada (now Ontario) and Lower Canada (Québec), even though Ontario seems "lower" on a map. In actuality, the directional riddle is easily solved: The names come from the flowing direction of the St. Lawrence River. The river flows from the Great Lakes "down" to the Atlantic Ocean, so Upper Canada included the present-day province of Ontario.

DEVELOPMENT OF THE DOMINION OF CANADA: 1812 THROUGH 1867

British North American colonies continued to increase in population after the migration of the United Empire Loyalists. Settlers were arriving in large numbers from Ireland, Scotland, England, and Germany. In 1812, settlers from Scotland and Ireland also began to arrive in the Red River Valley near present-day Winnipeg, Manitoba, to farm the rich, fertile land.

Meanwhile, on the eastern coast, the British colonies had become involved with the United States in the War of 1812. The empire-broadening hopes of U.S. President George Washington were shattered when colonists joined British military forces to defeat the American army. As time went on, it became too expensive for the British to keep defending Canada. It was also increasingly difficult to govern Canada from a distance. Another change was on the horizon.

As in the past, "Canadians" were still pushing to the Pacific Ocean in search of water routes and territory. Simon Fraser, son of a Loyalist family who had earlier sought refuge in Canada, explored the waterway that would eventually be named in his honor. Alexander Mackenzie earned the distinction of exploring the extensive river system (including tributaries) now known as the Mackenzie River in his search for the Northwest Passage. Exploration and mapping were occurring across the continent. Differing views were being expressed about the opportune vision of the Dominion of Canada's future.

John A. Macdonald, who would become the first Prime Minister and later Sir John A. Macdonald, believed the future of Canada lay in joining as one expansive country from coast to coast to coast. After much debate among involved leaders, the land was finally joined together as the Dominion of Canada. This was accomplished under the British North America Act on July 1, 1867. Strikingly, no revolution or war was necessary at that time for Canada to gain her independent status.

WESTWARD EXPANSION: 1867 THROUGH THE 1890s

In 1869, Canada purchased Rupert's Land from the Hudson's Bay Company, and greatly increased its size. The purchase was upsetting to the native people and the *Métis* (people of both French and native descent) who were living there. Of concern was the government failure to allow the Métis' land rights. As settlers began to move to this newly recognized area, the Métis felt threatened. They believed the arrival of settlers would drastically alter their way of life and property ownership. Louis Riel, a Métis leader, led a rebellion at Upper Fort Garry (Winnipeg). The Métis declared themselves the provisional government for the territory. To defuse the matter, the Canadian government passed the Manitoba Act of 1870. This Act created the fifth province, Manitoba, and guaranteed the Métis both property and language rights. During the next 15 years, Riel experienced a series of personal and public conflicts. His eventual hanging caused an outburst of racial tension between French/Native Canadians and

English Canadians, thus straining Canada's developing unity in this region.

How would *you* encourage hundreds of thousands of immigrants to settle on the expansive prairies of Canada and other less-populated areas? The Canadian Pacific Railroad knew the answer: Build a transcontinental railroad. The hard work and financial struggles that would be involved in such a process caused several interruptions in the building of the railway. Yet, just the *promise* of a transcontinental railroad linking to the opposite, eastern coast of Canada encouraged British Columbia to join the Canadian confederation. British Columbia would become the sixth province of Canada in 1871, before the railroad had even been completed.

In 1885, the dreams of a transcontinental railroad were finally achieved. For the first time in its youthful status as a country, a transportation route finally linked Canada from east to west. The Canadian Shield's craggy landscape and the piercing of the towering barrier of the Cordillera had proved most difficult for those building the railroad. The efforts of more than 15,000 Chinese workers helped thousands of others to accomplish the task of completing the railroad through the mountains of British Columbia. As the rails progressed across the prairies and climbed the mountains, thousands of settlers were arriving. The Canadian Pacific Railroad brought western Canada to life as villages and towns bustled in growth. Another rush, this time for gold, would change the mainland of British Columbia forever.

When the 1860 Cariboo Gold Rush had "evaporated," along with dreams of instant wealth, roads already had been built to the gold fields. These roads reached into the Cariboo Mountains of British Columbia, away from the more settled coastal areas. This opened up the mainland of the province to settlement. Similar happenings took place in the 1890s when the Klondike Gold Rush sparkled in the Yukon.

Toward the end of the 1800s, immigration was on the rise. To encourage the new immigrants to settle in the less-populated prairies and other areas, the Canadian Pacific Railroad began construction of the transcontinental railroad. In 1885, the railroad was complete, and towns began to spring up in unpopulated areas of western Canada.

ENTERING THE 20TH AND 21ST CENTURIES

Proud and confident, Canada greeted the twentieth century with jubilation. Immigrant populations had swelled the previously sparsely populated provinces. Canada, as a confederation, was establishing itself as an industrial and agricultural power.

The struggles of World War I and World War II called for

courage. Canadians responded with military manpower and precious natural resources to produce war materials. The contributions in time of war bolstered Canada's international stature and affirmed Canadian capabilities as a modern and industrial nation.

Between these wars, economic and social disasters resulting from the Great Depression tested Canadians' courage. In the years following these struggles of war and the economic depression, the standard of living increased for many people and the economy continued to expand. The latter portion of the twentieth century saw a vocal minority calling for Québec's *secession* (withdrawal) from the confederation of Canada. It wouldn't be the first time that Québec would be thinking independently. In 1982, the British Parliament approved the Constitution Act. This act *repatriated* (brought home) Canada's constitution from British Parliament (against Québec's objections.) This repatriation meant that Canada was now free to interpret and amend the constitution without deferring to the British Parliament. More recently, a 1995 referendum (the second) saw Québec voters just narrowly reject secession.

Recent years have experienced financial conflicts between federal and provincial systems. For example, matters of education and health care funding are largely the responsibility of individual provinces and territories. Decreases in "transfer payments" from the federal government have led to provincial and territorial struggles with health care and educational needs of the citizens, young and old. Recently developed political parties, such as the Bloc Québecois (represented only in Québec) and Reform Party, have promoted their special interests in political issues. These parties are in addition to the Liberal, Conservative, and New Democratic Parties already established in Canada. Economic issues within North America, including NAFTA (North American Free Trade Agreement, concerning trade among Canada, the United

States, and Mexico) continue to swirl about on a regular basis. (And yes, the Toronto Blue Jays once did win back-to-back World Series (baseball) championships!)

Canada's geographical and political map changed on April 1, 1999, when Nunavut was officially named Canada's third territory. Meaning "our land" in Inuktitut, the Inuit language, Nunavut was formed from the eastern portion of the Northwest Territories. This vast territory makes up one-fifth of Canada's size! Here, the Inuit way of life is now represented from within. Nunavut is self-governed by the Inuit, who comprise 85 percent of the population living there. (According to the 2001 census, Nunavut's population was 26,745; the census is taken every five years.) Fascinating, frustrating, tremendous, turbulent—will these descriptions of Canada's past also be descriptions of its future?

Painted faces sport maple leaves to mark Canada Day, which is celebrated on July 1. All sorts of merriment mark the 1867 formation of the Dominion of Canada, often including fireworks, picnics, parades, and other patriotic events.

Faces and Places

F ew people are permanent residents of any one place. *Migration* (movement from one location to another) occurs for various reasons for various people and involves a host of *push-and-pull* factors. Push-and-pull factors are those reasons why a person feels "pushed" from a present home and "pulled" to the attracting qualities of a different home. Consider factors of push-and-pull as you read about Canada's population and settlement clusters in this chapter.

INCREASED NUMBERS OF PERMANENT SETTLEMENTS

In Canada's early history, fur trading and fishing influenced European settlement patterns. Neither industry required large permanently settled population bases, although growing permanent settlements such as Québec City and Montréal did exist. The fur trade industry operated efficiently with expansive numbers of mobile (free-to-move) trappers and explorers. In the financially developing fisheries of historical Canada, many fishermen came seasonally to North America for their work and then returned to Europe. Not having to maintain permanent settlements for the fishermen kept profits for the fishing industry at a higher level. Push-and-pull factors were at work here.

Thus, as time progressed, the population grew more slowly than the agricultural and industrial population of the 13 colonies of the United States. As mentioned previously, this population difference was evident when the conflict of the French and Indian War occurred. Canadian settlement patterns evolved over time. Fur trading posts grew into established populations. The seigneurial system of farming stabilized and strengthened agricultural settlements in Québec. The transcontinental railroad brought many eager settlers to central and western Canada with dreams of establishing family farms. The growing number of permanent settlements, increasing immigrant populations, and expanding industries such as fishing, mining, and lumbering brought increases in numbers of urban dwellers over time. Today, nearly 80 percent of Canadians live in urban areas (communities with populations of 10,000 people or more).

POPULATION AND SETTLEMENT

As determined by the 2001 census, Canada's population is 30,007,094. This shows a growth of 4 percent (one of the smallest census-to-census growth rates Canada has experienced) since the 1996 census. As an interesting comparison, the city of Tokyo, Japan, has a population of only a few million fewer people than the entire country of Canada.

A significant population growth of 10 percent occurred in Alberta over the past five years. This increase is due to Alberta's booming economy, most notably along the

Edmonton-Calgary corridor. Much of this growth was *interprovincial* (population movement between provinces). An increase was also recorded in the province of Ontario, which had 6 percent growth. These arrivals were particularly visible in the "Golden Horseshoe" running through Toronto—with Toronto as an anchor, this horseshoe-shaped cluster of cities spreads along the shore of western Lake Ontario between Oshawa and St. Catharines. Much of Canada's manufacturing and service-related industry is located in this densely populated region. In fact, the horseshoe has grown to the north and west, and it now includes growing cities in the region extending from Barrie to Windsor (the "Windsor corridor extended horseshoe"). Push-and-pull factors occur at a dizzying speed in this densely populated region.

Cultural diffusion (the spreading of cultural traits from a point of origin over a larger area) is evident in the colorful clothing styles, art, music, delicious cuisines, and celebrated traditions throughout this region. People proudly share their heritages—unique to the countries from which they have moved. Walking through the Kensington Market area in Toronto, there is a riot of spectacular sights, smells, and sounds of the neighborhood. Here, pulsing action offers everything from coconut milk (enjoyed directly from the coconut with the aid of a straw through an opening in the shell) to airy fabrics to rhythmic sounds of global music. Such multicultural enrichment has also taken place in the bustling city of Montréal, the second-largest city in Canada, which is located on a 30-mile-long (48-kilometer-long) island in the St. Lawrence River.

Vancouver, too, offers diverse cultural delights. British Columbia saw a provincial increase of nearly 5 percent in population, with much of its growth occurring in the Lower Mainland and southwestern Vancouver Island. International immigrations are responsible for the majority of this growth. In fact, 75 percent of British Columbia's growth was from

Asian populations, particularly from India, Hong Kong, China, and Taiwan. Many of these Asian immigrants settle in the Vancouver and Richmond areas. Unlike much of the Asian population, the newcomers from India are more likely to settle in destinations outside of these two cities and even away from the lower mainland areas: Surrey and Abbotsford are home to approximately 40 percent of the Indian population. The choice of settlement areas may be related to the fact that a higher proportion of Indian immigrants are involved in manufacturing and agricultural industries. As is true in other Canadian cities with colossal immigrant populations, the reuniting of families has been a main theme in Canadian immigration policy.

The territory of Nunavut recognized an 8 percent growth in population. High birth rates occur among the Inuit. This, in combination with development in the capital city of Iqaluit, has raised the territory's population.

Along with the valued growth in Canada, declines in population have also come about. Population declines occurred in areas with resource-based economies such as northern Québec, although the Greater Montréal area of Québec showed an increased population. Newfoundland and the Yukon Territory experienced the emigration (moving away) of people to other provinces in Canada, as did the Northwest Territories. Overall, the six provinces of Prince Edward Island, Nova Scotia, New Brunswick, Québec, Manitoba, and Saskatchewan have remained quite stable in their population.

SOURCE OF POPULATION GROWTH

The main source of population growth for Canada as a whole results from immigration. More than one-half of the immigrants who came to Canada between 1996 and 2001 settled in Ontario. This influence is most remarkable in the global fabric of Toronto. With a population of 4.6 million (nearly one of every seven Canadians lives in this sprawling city),

Chinatown in Toronto is only one example of the multicultural environment this city has to offer. More than half of Toronto's residents are "minorities," even though they actually outnumber the Canadians! Almost 170 countries are represented in Toronto's diverse population, and more than 100 different languages are spoken.

foreign-born residents make up more than 50 percent of Toronto's population. Thus, minorities now compose the majority of Toronto's population! Every year more than 70,000 immigrants and refugees add diversity to the cultural mosaic of Toronto. Toronto's citizens come from nearly 170 countries and speak more than 100 languages. This kaleidoscope of cultures is evident in the splendid aromas and tastes of global foods, new ideas, world economic connections, and cultural richness of the city. Unfortunately, ethnic conflict and pressure on social services and language training also are visible within the cultural landscape of this vibrant city.

The federal government is committed to holding the immigration level at 1 percent of the population per year. With a present population of approximately 30 million, this means a goal of 300,000 new immigrants for the current year. The higher numbers of immigrants who tend to settle there challenge larger cities. Health and education services feel the pressure of such increases. Infrastructure supports (such as highways, water and sewer systems, and electricity) are striving to keep pace with population demands. Housing and transportation accommodations feel the strain of increased populations. Job opportunities—and attaining the qualifications for those jobs—are additional issues of concern.

Less-populated provinces, however, are eager to attract *more* immigrants to both rural and urban areas. This desire has the potential to improve the provinces' (and territories') economic base and help them experience gains in population. Finding the balance between attaining these preferred immigrant populations and providing necessary support services is a work in progress for Canada.

POPULATION DENSITY

As mentioned in Chapter 2, the majority of Canada's population lives in the narrow belt of land bordering the United States. Nearly 90 percent of Canada's population lives within 100 miles of the Canadian/U.S. border.

Population density refers to the number of people living per unit of land area—such as a square mile or square kilometer. (Canadians use a mixture of metric and imperial measurements in Canada, even though the official measurement system is metric.) The population density for the country of Canada is approximately 8.7 people per square mile (3 per square kilometer). This ranks Canada among the world's lowest population densities. The measure seems to indicate that fewer than nine people live on each square mile of Canadian land, but this statistic is misleading: Population settlements are not evenly distributed. There are crowded urban areas, where the population density is much higher, as well as more open, less-populated vistas. Clusters of cities, communities, and villages are interspersed with farms and physically isolated settlements. It is this variety on the canvas of Canada's landscape that offers a multitude of choices for the residents.

Rural areas and small towns account for 20 percent of Canada's population. Growth in these rural areas and communities since the last census depended on the proportion of residents who commuted to larger urban areas for work. Where the proportion was high, growth occurred, mainly as a result of people moving just beyond urban boundaries to live in a more rural setting.

Urban areas, home to 80 percent of Canada's population, are seeing population shifts as well. The city of Vancouver, British Columbia, has a population density of 11,545 people per square mile. Moving east, Toronto has a population density of more than 16,000 people per square mile. These high-density areas have many people living in multidwelling, high-rise housing complexes. In the eastern province of Nova Scotia, the city of Halifax has 150 people per square mile. These cities present a sampling of the vast range of population densities for urban areas in Canada. Yet, population distributions in rural areas may leave miles of sweeping space between you and the nearest neighbor!

MULTICULTURALISM

Multiculturalism (many cultures or ways of life) is a characteristic often used to describe Canadian society. French, British, and Aboriginal origins comprise approximately three-fifths of the country's population. The ethnicity and nationality of Canada is represented in the remaining two-fifths of the population. *Nationality* refers to a "belonging" or sense of self-identity when asked, "What are you?" *Ethnicity* is a bit more difficult to define. It refers to a group of people living as a minority population within a larger culture. An example of this is the ethnic area known as "Little Italy" in Toronto.

In 1971, Canada became the first country in the world to adopt a policy of multiculturalism. A subsequent, powerful legislative policy that followed in 1988 is known as the *Canadian Multiculturalism Act.* This policy affirmed Canada's recognition and value of its rich ethnic diversity. In 1997, the Department of Canadian Heritage restructured and renewed the multiculturalistic program. Three main goals offer focus for the program. One goal is that of identity—fostering a sense of belonging and attachment to Canada. Another goal is civic participation. Developing citizens who are active in their community and country will be instrumental in shaping the future of Canada. The third goal concerns social justice—building a country that respects and treats people of all origins fairly. By recognizing and celebrating Canada's multiculturalism, it is hoped that common goals of belonging, sharing, and social justice will occur. This, in turn, will bring opportunity and economic prosperity to the citizens. It is a valuable investment in Canada's future.

LANGUAGES

Canada is a *bilingual* country: It has two official languages. The *Official Languages Act* makes both English and French official languages of Canada. English is the mother language of

French and English are both official languages of Canada. Although the majority—59 percent—of the population speaks English as its first language, French is the first language for another 23 percent. Therefore, all federal documents (including road signs) are printed in both French and English.

59 percent of Canadians, while French is the first language for 23 percent of the population. This official bilingualism is reflected in the use of the French language in federal domains such as Parliament, the court systems, and in all federally printed documents.

While French and English are both official languages in Canada, French is spoken almost exclusively in much of

Québec. A much smaller percentage of people speak French in other provinces and territories. For example, fewer than 3 percent of people in the western provinces are fluent in French.

French immersion programs are available in Canadian schools. These immersion programs offer students throughout Canada the opportunity to study and learn in the French language. Participation varies according to one's location in Canada. It also varies according to grade levels in schools where French immersion is offered. Communities seeing benefits of bilingualism in the future work force and in the economic base offer more support for participation in French immersion programs.

As mentioned previously, more than 100 languages can be heard when traveling in Toronto and throughout Canada. As a sampling, in one city, you might hear Chinese, Italian, Punjabi, Spanish, Portuguese, Polish, German, Vietnamese, Arabic, Tagalog (Filipino), Greek, Cree, Ukrainian, Hindi, and Inuktitut!

Languages are as unique as they are abundant in Canada. For instance, in the Arctic North, *aya-yait* songs of the Inuit act as spoken maps for the often-deceiving landscape. There, even the wind patterns in the snow communicate the path to your destination if you listen and look observantly.

RELIGION

Christianity accounts for over 80 percent of religious affiliations in Canada. Of those people, 46 percent are Roman Catholic and 36 percent are Protestant. Most Christian Canadians of French descent are Roman Catholic, while most British descendents are Protestant.

Early French settlers were devout Roman Catholics, hoping to convert the native peoples already living there to Roman Catholicism. Much of the devotion has lessened in the modern age as church-attendance records, especially in

Québec, continue to decline. The French presence of the dominant Roman Catholic religion can be seen in architecture throughout portions of eastern Canada. Tiny French villages in Québec and New Brunswick have majestic stone churches with glistening tin roofs and ornate interiors. The Notre Dame Basilica, Montréal's oldest and grandest Catholic church, offers magnificent stained-glass windows and intricately carved wood in the interior.

The religious makeup of Canada is diversifying (becoming more varied) along with the faces of its population. Immigration patterns over the years have produced an increase in the faiths of Judaism, Muslim, Hinduism, Sikhism, and Buddhism. As affiliations grow, lessen, and change, Canada's religious composition reflects the diverse people who live there.

ABORIGINAL PEOPLES

Aboriginal peoples were the first inhabitants of the land area now known as Canada. Their survival, in every location on the land, depended on respect for the environment, sharing, and cooperation. Descendents of these original dwellers have passed spiritual beliefs and cultural traditions from generation to generation.

The Constitution Act of 1982 recognizes three main groups of Aboriginal Peoples: the First Nations (formerly referred to as "Indians"), the Métis, and the Inuit. About 3 percent of the Canadian population is currently recognized as Aboriginal. The majority (69 percent) of Aboriginal Peoples are First Nations; Métis comprise 26 percent; the Inuit, 5 percent of these Aboriginal populations.

First Nations

The people of the First Nations are as varied as the landscapes on which they lived. Along the west coast, the resource-rich waters brought a bounty of salmon, shellfish, and whales.

These plentiful resources made permanent settlements possible for coastal people. Leisure time allowed for the carving of cedar and stone into elegant objects of art, including huge totem poles, some of which can be seen in museums throughout the world today.

In the wide expanses of the prairie, families cooperated in hunting migratory buffalo. The buffalo supplied food, tools, clothing, and hides for the easily transported tepees used as the families' homes. The nomadic Woodland First Nations, Iroquoian farmers of southeastern Ontario, and hunting groups of the First Nations in the Mackenzie and Yukon River basins each had distinct cultures. These Aboriginal cultures were based on the peoples' spiritual connection to the land and the life forms it supported. Today, more than one-half of the First Nations peoples live on *reserves*, sections of land set aside for Aboriginal Peoples.

Métis

The Métis are descendents of French fur traders who married First Nations women. The Métis (a French word meaning "mixed") developed their own distinct culture on the prairies. The open prairie had been the buffalo hunting grounds of the Métis for hundreds of years, but farms built by settlers and the transcontinental railroad cars that brought farmers' wheat to market changed the traditional ways of life for the Métis.

Inuit

The Inuit lived and settled throughout northern regions of Canada. The majority of the Inuit population still lives there today. Historically, hunting seals, whales, caribou, and polar bears provided means of survival for the people. Today, some Inuit still hunt for food and clothing resources in traditional ways.

An important tool created by the Inuit was the *inuksuk*, a

This Inuit man is covering the opening to his *iglu* (igloo). The snow figure in the shape of a man is called an *inuksuk*. It is a landmark used to orient travel on an otherwise barren landscape.The Inuit are indigenous to northern Canada, and some still live traditionally in the Nunavut territory. Historically, the Inuit survived by hunting seals, whales, caribou, and polar bears in the frigid Northwest Territories.

stone figure placed on the physical landscape. The term *inuksuk* (plural, *inuksuit*) means "to act in the capacity of a human." These stone monuments were placed on the mystifying land to guide people as they journeyed across the barren landscape devoid of physical landmarks. Inuksuit were also used as hunting aids. Attaching strands of wind-waving vegetation (such as arctic heather) around the necks of these stone statues, arranged in two wide rows, frightened the caribou and directed them between the rows to a more restricted hunting area. An inuksuk might also serve as a message center, mark a place where a sacred or significant event happened, or serve as a "road sign" for navigation through the northern lands.

Not only the physical landscape held inuksuit: Traditional legends, figures in string games played with children, and a winter constellation also hold images of inuksuit in spiritual landscapes for the Inuit today. Additionally, some inuksuit still remain as signatures upon the stark landscape of the North.

European Contacts with Aboriginal Peoples

When increased numbers of Europeans arrived in what is now Canada, aboriginal (native to an area) ways of life were changed forever. Contact with Europeans brought diseases previously unknown to the Aborigines. The contacts also brought guns and land treaties. These treaties granted certain rights and benefits to the Aboriginal Peoples in exchange for giving up titles (ownership) to the land. Certain rights to hunt, fish, and trap on ancestral lands are examples of the Aboriginal rights that were granted.

Today, the Canadian government and Aboriginal Peoples continue to negotiate new agreements for land and recognition of rights. Aboriginal leaders are acting to preserve their cultures and remaining traditional ways of life. After decades of persistence and dedication by these concerned leaders, the government and general public have an awareness of the once-free, self-sustaining nations of the Aboriginal Peoples. In seeking their own forms of government, such as the Inuit have done in the territory of Nunavut since 1999, Aboriginal peoples want to maintain the rich diversity of their traditional cultures. They hope, also, to assume their natural place in Canadian society.

This chapter began with historical considerations of push-and-pull factors. It is closing with the same concept in mind. Canada, a country with diversity in its faces and places, reflects the multiculturalism of its past and present. The role of government in Canada's policymaking for this diverse population will be discussed in the next chapter.

Canada's national government—Parliament—is run by the Prime Minister.
Parliament includes the House of Commons (301 elected members from
all regions throughout Canada), the Senate (104 members appointed by the
Prime Minister for life terms), and the Governor General, who represents
the Queen.

devastating effects. Aboriginal systems of government, already in place, were weakened. Aboriginal ways of life were threatened, and the recognition of Aboriginal rights was vanishing quickly.

As awareness for these past circumstances continues to become heightened today, federal and provincial governments are working together with Aboriginal peoples. They hope to reestablish recognition of the Aboriginals' self-governing heritage.

Having the power to govern their own population, the Aboriginal peoples will be in a better position to decide on matters affecting their unique lives and ways of the land. Since the 1990s, the federal government has been earnest in developing the process for self-government. Meetings with Aboriginal leaders at the federal, regional, and local levels have taken place. Under self-government, the differing Aboriginal groups will shape their own political, cultural, and economic circumstances. Provincial and territorial governments will become involved when their interests or jurisdictions are affected. Overriding laws at the federal level, such as the Criminal Code, will prevail.

One Aboriginal group has achieved self-government status. The territorial governing of Nunavut offers visionary distinctions as progress is made in this historical role.

GOVERNING NUNAVUT

Nunavut was previously governed from afar. Although a part of the Northwest Territories since 1870, the Inuit who live there sent no elected representative to the territorial government until 1966. In fact, it was only in 1960 that Aboriginal peoples in Canada received the right to vote in federal elections. The Inuit have campaigned since that time for land, mineral, and constitutional rights.

A shift in living from the land to living in settlements occurred when the Canadian government began providing

The territory of Nunavut is Inuit-led; it is one of the first worldwide examples of an indigenous self-governing population. Although the Inuit maintain a distinctly different culture, they are still very much a part of Canada's multicultural makeup.

education, health care, and housing. Parental desire for children to learn English as they attended school added momentum for the movement into settlements. The decline in the use of Inuktitut (Inuit language) was also affected by the satellite-available television that brought CBC (Canadian Broadcasting Corporation) and "Hockey Night in Canada" to remote Arctic villages.

Along with the cultural changes, social and political changes also came. The Inuit traits of patience, acceptance, and enduring confidence that had ensured survival in the past benefited the quest for self-government in the future.

Years of planning and negotiation, along with precedent-setting Native Claims settlements (government return of limited land and resource claims to native populations), were essential to this transition of government.

Under the 1993 Nunavut Land Claims Agreement Act, the Inuit received a settlement of $1.1 billion (Canadian Dollars). This compensation from the federal government is being paid over a 14-year period. (The money is being held "in trust," or in reserve for future use, with the interest money being used for scholarships and business financing, along with other developmental plans.) The Inuit also gained control of approximately 18 percent of the land, including mineral rights in a carefully selected 10 percent of that land portion. In exchange for hunting rights, a share of resource royalties (from oil, gas, and mineral development), and greater roles in managing the land and environment, the Inuit signed away future aboriginal claims to all remaining lands and water in Nunavut.

The recently created, Inuit-governed territory of Nunavut faces many challenges. High levels of unemployment, low education levels, high costs for goods and public services, and high substance-abuse rates are issues being faced in the 28 scattered communities of Nunavut. Its residents will be responsible for education, health, social services, language, and culture, among other areas of responsibilities. Governmental agencies for these departments will be located in 10 communities away from the headquartered capital of Iqaluit (located on Baffin Island). This is being done to ensure access to services and jobs throughout the extensive territory.

Inuit values and beliefs are being incorporated into the contemporary system of government. The working language of Nunavut's government is Inuktitut, along with English, French, and Inuinnaqtun (a distinctive dialect spoken in the western portion of the Kitikmeot region). Inuktitut is being promoted throughout the educational system in the teachings of culture, traditions, and heritage.

Nunavut's economic future is strongly linked to its natural resources. Mining, petroleum development, commercial fishing, hunting, and ecotourism are ventures of opportunity. By moving forward into the future while still acknowledging the traditions and teachings of the past, the people of Nunavut remain determined. They are determined to maintain a distinct cultural community—not as a separate sovereignty, but within multiculturalistic Canada.

THE ROLE OF GOVERNMENT IN EDUCATION

Unlike most industrialized countries, Canada has no federal education system. Rather, education in Canada consists of ten provincial and three territorial systems. Public schools, "separate" (denominational) schools, and private schools offer comprehensive educational opportunities for all students. The Constitution Act authorized each province and territory to be responsible for its own educational system. While similar in many ways, the curriculum of each provincial system reflects its particular history, culture, and region.

The Canadian government provides partial financial assistance for provincial education in the form of transfer payments. These funds, transferred from the federal government to the provincial government according to strict qualifications, are becoming more and more restricted as the economy changes. Substantial government subsidies (financial support) keep university and non-university (technical and community colleges) expenses to a somewhat attainable level. Financial commitments from the government rank Canada among the world leaders in public education funding per student. But this, too, is changing as fiscal responsibility restricts money flows.

Combining school boards and school partnerships with private businesses are two examples of cost-reducing measures being taken throughout Canada. Reform of provincial educational systems and increased accountability for ensured learning success are modifications being made to attain federal transfer payments. As with most democratic societies today, streamlined services are essential to the overall maintenance of such vitally important institutions. Streamlining of Canada's health care system is another governmental challenge for the country.

THE ROLE OF GOVERNMENT IN HEALTH CARE

The future of Canada's health care system is a crucial concern to the people living in this land of socialized medicine. Under the socialized system, the government assumes financial responsibility for the health care of all Canadians. Questions of funding and mounting pressure to use new (and more expensive) technologies affect every province and territory. While the need for reform is widely recognized, the route for reform poses difficult questions.

In the late 1950s, Canadians hoped to improve public health and eliminate disparities among those receiving care. Whether one was poor, wealthy, or anywhere in between, it was desired that health care be available for all. To achieve this goal, provinces were legislated by the federal government to set up health insurance plans for every Canadian. Although health insurance plans have not reduced health problems, they have increased security that health care is available for people with low incomes and those with serious illnesses. Economic disruption, however, has forced provincial governments to carefully examine their finances in order to balance budgets.

Under the *Canada Act*, the federal government pays a share of health care costs to the provinces and territories. The government originally promised to cover half of the costs in return for meeting qualifications, but it is now contributing only about 15 percent. This change is critically straining budgets of the more-populated provinces. British Columbia, Alberta, and Ontario use nearly 40 percent of their total budgets to meet escalating health care needs. This funding issue will continue to get worse as more resources are needed to support an aging population.

Federal and provincial governments are in an awkward situation. Reform in health care spending must occur, or free health care will no longer be available for all Canadians. Faced with this crisis, plans are being discussed in several provinces to shift some payment responsibilities to patients by offering "user fee," or fee-based, services. In 2001, a poll showed that 60 percent of Canadians supported the expansion of private health care services and user fees. Yet, in that same poll, 75 percent of Canadians were also willing to make compromises, such as paying higher taxes, to maintain the present system assuring equal access for all to health care.

The transformation of Canada's health care system will not come easily or immediately. Provincial reform efforts, along with local health care networks, are striving to work toward the goal of equitable access for quality health care. This is a desired expectation of the public, and one that brings difficult questions. Difficult questions also arise from the ongoing issue of Québec's desire to secede (separate) from Canada.

SECESSION OF QUÉBEC

For 35 years, a political struggle has been occurring between the *Parti Québecois* and the rest of the Canadian government. This political party is dedicated to the *secession* (separation) of Québec from the rest of Canada. They feel this "sovereign (independent) association" with Canada would allow for the preservation of the French Canadian culture and French language that offer a sense of identity for Québec.

For many years Canada has struggled with the question of national unity versus Québec's secession/independence. The separatists feel that secession from Canada would preserve the French-Canadian culture so prevalent within Québec; others who are against secession feel the country should remain a united whole.

A centuries-long history of Francophone (French-speaking) vs. Anglophone (English-speaking) rivalry continues to drive debate. You may recall the battle on the Plains of Abraham where Québec City fell to the British. This was followed by the Treaty of Paris in 1763, requiring New France to surrender to the British.

While many in Québec favor secession, not all people living in Québec want to secede. The Aboriginal peoples of northern Québec, many of the English-speaking minority (and even some of the French), and most recent immigrants are strongly opposed to the separatist movement.

In 1980, the first of two referendums (a vote on an issue being referred to the federal government) was held in Québec. The referendum sought to allow the provincial government to negotiate "sovereign-association" status with Canada. The referendum was defeated, 60 percent to 40 percent. The Parti Québecois had lost. One reason was that older citizens felt threatened by the possible outcomes a separatist change would bring. A considerable Anglophone voting population also affected the outcome.

Attempts to reconcile opposing views of the separatist issue accomplished little between the first and second referendums. Not only were many Canadians, including some residents of Québec, frustrated with the amount of time, money, and energy being consumed in this issue, but economic and social progress were also being affected. An emotional second referendum took place in 1995. This referendum asked the people of Québec to vote yes or no with regard to the question, "Should Québec become sovereign?" The by-a-whisker vote was extremely close: 51 percent voted no, and 49 percent voted yes.

Following the failure of two referendums, the *Québec Secession Reference* (1996) was heard by Canada's Supreme Court. This procedure refers legal and factual questions of importance for the Canadian government to the Supreme Court. Three questions of importance were asked with regard to the possibility of Québec's secession. The Supreme Court ruled that a province could not *unilaterally* (one side only decides) secede; there had to be agreement among governing Canadians. The Supreme Court also ruled that any secession would require an amendment to the Constitution.

This would be drastically difficult for the entire government of Canada to agree to. Another ruling stated that a "clear majority" would have to support secession with a clearly stated question (not an ambiguous one, as in the past) being asked. Later legislation (the Clarity Act of June 2000) set conditions for negotiation prior to the vote if Québec holds another referendum on secession.

The outcome of this divisive issue is by no means settled. Does Québec hold the illusion that it can separate without Canada's consent? Only time will tell. Meanwhile, Québec's economy must be looked after, regardless of the ongoing issue of secession. Abundant natural resources and hydroelectricity are aspects of Québec's economy that need attention and care. You will read more about Québec's economy and the economy of Canada in the next chapter.

While rural scenes like this one seem almost a throwback to simpler times, Canadians who live in rural areas—one-fifth of Canada's population—know that this is much more than an old-fashioned way of life. Canada is a major supplier of agricultural products, especially wheat, to much of the world.

CHAPTER

6

Economy

For seven consecutive years—from 1994 to 2000—Canada held the distinction of being the best country in the world in which to live. The annual ranking by the United Nations assesses such things as life expectancy, adult literacy, and economic prosperity. Canada's life expectancy is 79 years, with a literacy rate of 97 percent. These high standards of living combine with the high-tech industrial society of Canada to make it an economic competitor in the global economy. In this chapter we will explore some of the economic successes Canada is presently maintaining.

LINKING CANADIANS TO THE WORLD

Being the second-largest country in the world posed many communication difficulties until recent decades. The successful launch of the Canadian Anik A1 communications satellite in 1972 was a first step in linking people from all corners of Canada. This achievement established the country as a world leader in satellite technology. It made Canadians pioneers in what has developed into a lucrative industry for the country.

Satellite communications ensure that all Canadians have access to the most recent communications and services. This infrastructure has the promise to increase efficiency, reduce cost, and improve public and social services—especially in rural and remote areas. Cost-effective education, health, and e-commerce services can be transmitted to the most physically remote locations in Canada.

The Canadian Space Agency's satellite communications program is also bringing international economic benefits to the country. Expertise and developing technology of this program are securing a place in the global economy for Canada. Being able to access a view of the world through an electronic window continues to open new opportunities. One such opportunity is that of the "Canadarm" technology.

The Canadarm was first launched into space in 1981 with the *Columbia* space shuttle. Its success on that mission secured a position in the future of space technology. Canadarm2 traveled to the International Space Station on the *Endeavor* space shuttle in 2001. This robotic arm is capable of lifting heavy modules, weighing tons, to continue construction of the space station. It sits on a power-providing platform and is remotely "flown" like an airplane. A camera mounted on the end of the arm offers a space vision for the controller in the space station as well as the Canadian Space Agency ground center in Québec. This impressive camera checks to make sure outer surfaces of the space station are in healthy shape for future international dockings. Additionally, the arm flexes its muscle during mainte-nance and assembly phases of the International Space Station. In return for the technology of the Canadarm, Canada will continue to send astronauts to the Space Station and assist with its management. Who knows where Canada will go from here!

BACK ON EARTH: RURAL LANDSCAPES

When waking up to rural landscapes in Canada, a different way of life greets Canadians. Less hurried and often more casual than large cities, these areas are home to one-fifth of Canada's population. Rural Canadians offer significant contributions to the country's wealth and prosperity.

Exports of agricultural and agri-food products have reached an all-time high. By sending more products to more countries, Canada has proven that it is a global supplier of choice for international customers. While total numbers of farms in Canada have decreased, the average farm size, crop yields, and livestock numbers are increasing. Technological changes and innovations in agriculture, domestic and global economic factors, and changing consumer tastes are events and trends to which farmers are responding.

Only 7 percent of Canada's land area is utilized for agriculture. Most of this productive area is along the southern border of Canada. Wheat is the country's largest agricultural export. Many of the world's top pasta producers, such as Italy and Turkey, import voluminous quantities of Canadian durum wheat. Livestock productions of cattle and hogs have provided valuable export markets of beef and pork to several countries.

Canadians have also identified prominent issues of concern for these less-populated regions in which they live. Access to federal government programs and resources for community development, targeted opportunities for rural and Aboriginal youth, and partnerships for rural development are priority concerns. The *Canadian Rural Partnership,* a key federal framework for supporting rural communities, works to respond to such issues. The *"Rural Lens"* policy is a way of viewing federal issues through the eyes of Canadians earning a living from the land. Increased awareness for rural issues is happening because of federal programs such as these. By understanding the impact of new policies and programs on the lives of Canadians, it is hoped future initiatives will assess rural implications before legislative acts are passed.

Also of concern is the quality of life in rural areas. Receiving proper health care and educational services, in addition to economic and community benefits, will hopefully strengthen the decreasing numbers of Canadians living in these areas. By providing training, economic development, and strategic partnerships, smaller communities hope to be better equipped to compete in a global economy.

Increasing youth participation can play an important role in shaping a successful future for rural Canada. Young people are key to sustaining long-term economic and social development. They will be vital in building stable, vibrant communities for the future.

TOURISM

Many visitors come to Canada to view nature's breathtaking and unspoiled beauty. Visually magnificent and naturally diverse, Canada's 39 national parks weave through every province and territory.

By the dawn of the twenty-first century, tourism spending exceeded $54 billion (Canadian Dollars) a year—and was increasing annually. The United Kingdom, Japan, France, and Germany were at the top of the overseas visitor market, while United States residents were significant continental visitors. Sightseeing, at both natural landscapes and cultural heritage sites, and shopping top the list of visitor activities in Canada.

Ecotourism

Canada has become a favorite destination for whale watchers, birders, and nature photographers. A range of adventure travel, including hiking, canoeing, kayaking, and snowmobiling, offers additional choices for Canada's lucrative tourism industry. The Canadian wilderness has become a natural, financial resource for the tourism economy.

More and more tourists are flocking to Canada to enjoy the natural resources available for vacationers. Whale watching, birding, nature photography, hiking, rock climbing, fishing, canoeing, kayaking, and snowmobiling are among the popular ecotourism activities.

In Manitoba, scuba diving the clear, cold depths of ancient glacial-formed lakes is an adventue for some ecotourists. Clinging to granite faces reaching a quarter-mile into the sky in the Cordillera of British Columbia offers an adrenaline rush for rock climbers of all ages. In areas of cold climate, you can tiptoe across an aluminum ladder spanning a deep, yawning, glacial crevasse. Twice each day, New Brunswick's Bay of Fundy offers the marvel of the greatest tides on earth: At low tide, you can literally walk on the ocean floor, and the high tide rolls in 50 feet higher (roughly the same height as a four-story building). Rich feeding grounds in this region also make it one of the world's most accessible sites for viewing marine animals such as whales.

Shopping

Of course, there are numerous shopping opportunities in the large cities of Canada such as Vancouver, Toronto, and Montréal. In addition, at eight city blocks long by three city blocks wide, the

West Edmonton Mall in Alberta holds the record for the world's largest shopping and entertainment center—more than 800 stores, in addition to services and attractions located inside the mall, offer respite for Canadians and visitors alike. Submarine rides, a zoo, the world's largest indoor "lake," a roller coaster, an NHL-size hockey rink, and fantasy-themed hotels are just a few of the sights to be seen in this megacomplex.

West Edmonton Mall's location may seem unlikely—it attracts million of visitors and generates multimillions of dollars in revenue. Why? Spurred by petroleum production, the city of Edmonton has become a huge regional economic hub with a population exceeding 1 million. But ask any Albertan on a brutal winter day, when a kicking wind swirls snow all around, and you will really begin to understand the appeal of an indoor mall!

RESOURCE-BASED INDUSTRIES

The abundance of natural resources in Canada has helped make it a leading industrial exporter. Products from the mining, energy, and forestry industries are major exports for the Canadian economy. Energy production from petroleum, natural gas, and hydroelectricity also account for export income from resource-based industry.

Coal and uranium provide one-third of Canada's electrical power. Hydroelectric facilities are also a source of energy for many Canadians. This energy resource allows Canada to generate electricity without producing harmful emissions that pollute the air. Favorable water conditions have even allowed surplus hydroelectricity to be exported to the United States. The most extensive hydroelectric development occurs in the province of Québec. Much of the development in the northern part of the province, both existing and proposed, affects the Aboriginal Cree population living there. Numerous agreements, lawsuits, and settlements reflect the ongoing conflict stemming from hydro-electric development in this northern region.

Forests cover more than one-half of the Canadian landscape. They are important to Canada's economy and environment. Softwood lumber, wood pulp, and newsprint lead the list of forest industry exports. The climate-moderating forests act as natural air and water filters, while also producing employment opportunities for Canadians.

MANUFACTURING AND SERVICE INDUSTRIES

As the sixth-largest vehicle producer in the world, Canada's manufacturing industry continues to grow. The automotive parts and motor vehicle sector of this industry make it Canada's largest manufacturing contributor to the GDP (gross domestic product). The United States and Canada rely heavily on each other in the import and export trading segments of this industry.

Continuing advances in information and communication technologies have helped Canada's service industry to grow rapidly. Service industries in Canada's economy account for over two-thirds of the country's total GDP. Occupations in such service industries as accounting, architecture, health, marketing, and transportation, just to name a few, offer visible employment opportunities in Canada. Countries around the world are also benefiting from research and development technologies of the service industries.

Canada's top three trading partners are the United States, Japan, and the United Kingdom. With its abundant natural resources and skilled labor force, Canada enjoys solid economic relationships with these countries, as well as many others throughout the world. Some shadows loom over Canada's economy within the North American continent, however. Softwood lumber disputes and salmon "wars" with the United States add stress to the trading economies of these two countries. NAFTA (North American Free Trade Agreement) trade issues are also a source of challenge between Canada, the United States, and Mexico.

SOFTWOOD LUMBER DISPUTES

Sometimes another country can produce and sell goods for a lower cost than the industry can bear in one's home country. This "other" country then sells the product to the home country at a lower cost. For example, Canada provides softwood lumber to the United States for a lower price than the lumber can be manufactured there. To make up for this price difference, the United States government requires Canadian producers to pay hefty *duties* (fees) on softwood lumber that is imported from Canada. This added duty makes the price higher so that consumers are more likely to purchase lumber produced in the United States.

Long-standing disputes between Canada and the United States have occurred, and are still occurring, in the softwood lumber industry. As a result, thousands of jobs have been lost and more are at risk. The U.S. Commerce Department declares that Canadian lumber producers benefit from government subsidies because the Canadian government charges low fees to cut timber on public land. There is also the challenged fact that Canadian lumber is being sold in the United States below its fair market value. Because of these two issues, the imposed duty rates of between $2 and $3 billion (Canadian) per year were put in place to offset financial injuries to the U.S. lumber industry.

The concept of trying to "even the playing field" causes rippling effects for different segments of the softwood lumber industry. Construction workers needing a supply of softwood lumber to build new homes in the United States have to pay more for this product. Still, U.S. lumber producers are demanding even higher duties to offset any financial losses in their companies. Lumber workers in logging communities across Canada are losing jobs because their company's mill cannot afford to pay these duties. Lumber workers in the United States risk further job losses because their companies have difficulty competing with the lower-priced Canadian product.

Canada's softwood forests are a rich resource for lumber, an important part of Canada's economy. Because of duties (fees) that the United States charges Canada to sell lumber in the United States, the lumber industry has begun to suffer. The two countries, along with Mexico, are working on a trade agreement that will ensure a fair but competitive market for many goods and services.

It is hoped that reform for long-term markets will eventually result from this dispute. A fair yet competitive market for softwood lumber is important to the economies of both Canada and the United States. Seamless trading in the softwood lumber industry is not a practice that will come soon or easily to these two key economic trading partners.

SALMON WARS

What ownership problems could arise when a natural resource has the ability to move and relocate between two countries? Would both countries have access "rights" to the resource? Canada's natural resources of oil, natural gas, and forests are not able to perform this moving feat, but the natural resource of salmon certainly can—and does.

"Salmon wars" on the West Coast are long-running

between Canada and the United States. For years, the two countries have disagreed over who owns this financial resource of the coastal waters and what quantities of salmon can be harvested. Certain salmon species spawn (lay eggs) in Canadian rivers, so Canada believes ownership is theirs, not the fishermen's nets scooping up these species in Washington, Oregon, and Alaska. Fishing companies in the United States, however, believe they have access to the salmon when they are feeding and living in U.S. coastal waters.

Viewpoints of Aboriginal peoples, on both sides of the border, are also being voiced. Historically, the Aboriginal populations had built an entire culture and economy based on the salmon. Some communities would move hundreds of miles to harvest salmon during the summer run. Later, they would trade the fish with other Aboriginal communities in the interior lands. Eventually, the European societies in North America became aware of the abundance of salmon in the treasured waters. New markets opened and demand for salmon was high.

The Aboriginal communities, fishermen, and salmon canneries on both sides of the border soon discovered the once-extensive quantities of salmon were being reduced quickly. If conservation measures were not taken soon, the salmon supply was in danger of being depleted.

Attempts were made to come to an agreement over quotas of how many fish could be harvested by people living in Canada and the United States. Agreeing to stop overfishing the coastal waters would hopefully bring some stability to the salmon population and industry. Disputes and varying forms of treaties have attempted to resolve the situation. A Pacific Salmon Treaty was signed with hopes to remedy the disputes. It aimed to provide conservation policies to protect and rebuild salmon spawning grounds. The treaty also worked to redistribute quotas of salmon species available to be caught for both countries. Following the treaty objectives has been a difficult path.

At stake is not only an industry worth hundreds of millions of dollars annually, but also the ways of life for thousands of fishermen, their families, and coastal communities.

NAFTA—THE NORTH AMERICAN FREE TRADE AGREEMENT

In an effort to create a mechanism to resolve disputes and provide "free trade" on the continent of North America, the governments of Canada, the United States, and Mexico created NAFTA. NAFTA went into effect on January 1, 1994. The intent of the international agreement was to eliminate tariffs (fees added to the value) on imported and exported goods between the three countries. An additional purpose of this legislation was to remove certain quotas in order to improve trade among the three partners.

Procession of the NAFTA legislation is occurring gradually over a 5- to 15-year period in order to give each industry time to adjust to this more level playing field. During this time, individual industries are striving to improve efficiency to compete with trading industries among the three countries. Each country has specific strengths upon which to build and retrain its work force. As jobs were lost in ineffective industries, they were gained in the effective, stronger industries. This has resulted in a "continental" village of producers, rather than each country attempting to produce many things it needs on its own. NAFTA also allows Canada, the United States, and Mexico to discuss environmental effects of the trade agreement.

Will the countries' specializations and trade benefit all parties? Will increased trade improve the economic welfare of Canada, the United States, and Mexico as proposed? The long-term progress of this agreement has widened the outlook of all three countries to include an expanded global village where changes will affect the way people earn a living. These changes will bring both positive and negative influences to the lives of people who reside in North America. Moreover, guarded concern for individual self-reliance of these countries still remains.

Montréal is the second-largest city in Canada. It is a bustling, multicultural city that blends old with new. More and more "pop culture" both comes from and is introduced to this centuries-old city.

7

Living in
Canada Today

C anadians are proud of their diverse heritage and achievements. Its proximity to the United States often means that they are perceived as similar societies, but the two countries do have many differences. Former Prime Minister Pierre Trudeau, highly esteemed by the Canadian public, once stated, "Americans should never underestimate the constant pressure on Canada which the mere presence of the United States has produced. We're different people *from* you, and we're different people *because* of you." This statement describes the complex influence the United States has on the Canadian sense of identity.

Observations of human diversity help to more clearly define the essence of one's culture. Knowledge, traditions, and behaviors can set people apart who may, at first glance, appear to be essentially similar. In this chapter, we will embark on a snapshot tour of life in Canada today. Celebrations and traditions, leisure activities, a portrait of

Canada's youth, Canadian and regional distinctions, and the environment all offer insight into the daily lives of Canadians in the twenty-first century.

CELEBRATIONS AND TRADITIONS

Canada celebrates many of the same holidays as the United States, especially religious holidays such as Easter and Christmas. In May, Canadians can also be found celebrating Queen Victoria's birthday, with gatherings of friends and family. This commemorative day, celebrated since 1845 in honor of then-reigning Queen Victoria of England, is viewed as the first of the summer holidays.

Celebrations large and small occur throughout Canada on July 1 for Canada Day. Fireworks, picnics, parades, and patriotic events commemorate the anniversary of the formation of the Dominion of Canada in 1867. Another public holiday, occurring the first weekend of August, is known as the August Civic Holiday. This is the next to last (with Labor Day still to come in September) of summer holidays. During this holiday, Canadians can often be found enjoying the luxury of the mountains, beaches, lakes, and beautiful outdoor scenery that the country is blessed with.

Canadian Thanksgiving is celebrated much as it is in the United States, except for an earlier date, reflecting the earlier end to the growing season further north. Celebrated on the second Monday of October in Canada, this autumnal event truly incorporates a bounty of harvest to be thankful for. Incredible shows of leaves changing colors, active harvesting of the land, and plates of turkey with all the trimmings indicate the presence of Thanksgiving.

INFLUENCES OF HEROES

A rich tapestry of heroes from both the past and present color Canadians' lives. Canada seems to recognize the achievements of these heroes with unassuming pride, rather than elevating them to almost superhero status. By examining Canada's heroes, one can better understand the attitudes and forces that have shaped this country. The creation of Canadian identity is a dynamic, changing process. People from all walks of life inspire and enrich the national character.

Consider the life of Canadian Terry Fox, a particularly inspirational Canadian. After losing his leg to cancer, he set the goal of running (with an artificial leg) across Canada from Newfoundland to British Columbia. His 1980 "Marathon of Hope" was a mission to raise funds and increase awareness for cancer research. Although Terry Fox's death prevented him from completing his mission, his legacy continues with the tradition of Terry Fox Runs that occur throughout Canada. Today, students and fellow Canadians partake in this annual September event that has raised more than $300 million (Canadian Dollars) worldwide for cancer research.

No matter where you look—science, law, Aboriginal Peoples, politics, religion, women, philosophy—the character and achievement of certain individuals have contributed to the identity of Canada.

LEISURE TIME

Canada's long winters, with freezing temperatures for most of the country, have played a significant role in the development of Canadian sports. Hockey, a sport that evolved from varied games played on ice, is a much-played and much-watched sport in Canada today. The first public ice hockey exhibition was played in 1875 on a rink in Montréal. Since then, many Canadian children (boys *and* girls) have taken hockey sticks to ice patches, quiet streets, playgrounds, and ice arenas with passion and hope. The passion of playing—or of being a spectator cheering for a favorite team—has made ice hockey the national winter sport of Canada. "Hockey Night in Canada" is a widely viewed Saturday evening event in many Canadian homes during hockey season. Speed and figure

Canada's long, cold winters have produced many wildly popular wintertime sports—including, of course, hockey. Canadians all over the country tune into "Hockey Night in Canada," a television show celebrating the national winter sport.

skating, skiing, snowboarding, and curling are also popular winter sports that many Canadians enjoy today.

A CANADIAN CULTURAL INSTITUTION

The Canadian Broadcasting Corporation, commonly known as the CBC, offers television and radio programming for countrywide enjoyment. Approximately 9 out of 10 people view CBC's television programming. More than one-half of adult Canadians listen to CBC's varied radio services. Operating in French and English, CBC radio and television networks offer informative and entertaining programs. Canadians love to laugh about their political happenings, even though they may be worrisome at times! A weekly TV show, "This Hour Has 22 Minutes," is viewed by more than 1 million people. Poking fun at politicians, headline makers, and news events, this successful TV series emphasizes humor in daily experiences.

CBC Radio provides marvelous broadcasts that discuss issues of relevance from all regions of Canada. Incredibly, you can tune your radio to CBC in the Atlantic Provinces and listen to your favorite radio hosts as you drive all the way to Vancouver, nearly some 4,000 miles to the west. Perhaps you'll hear the regional range of phone-in responses to "Cross-Country Checkup," Canada's open-line radio program. Broadcast every Sunday afternoon across Canada, lively discussions on issues of national interest or importance reflect a sampling of the ideas and thoughts of people living throughout this immense and highly diverse land. Listening to the cross-country dialogue is thought provoking—listeners can hear the shared perceptions and varied thinking of people living from coast to coast to coast!

POP CULTURE

Canada has captured worldwide attention with its incredible wealth of popular musicians. Celine Dion, Shania Twain, Sarah McLachlan, Alanis Morissette, Diana Krall, Loreena McKennit, Bryan Adams, and the Tragically Hip are just a few of the many vocal gifts from Canada.

Jim Carrey, Michael J. Fox, Donald and Kiefer Sutherland, and Dan Akroyd are talented performers who have been pulled across the border to the lucrative Hollywood movie industry of the United States. However, many movies and television shows are now being produced in Canada. Financially encouraged by government policies, Canada has become a popular shooting location for movies and television shows. The landscapes of the Canadian Rockies and transformation of such cities as Vancouver, Toronto, and Montréal are appearing more and more often in pop culture media. Along with Canadian movie and television performers, talented Canadian technicians and high-tech animation studios are affecting the balance in favor of Canadian influences in this industry.

CANADA'S YOUTH

With good news about the progress of Canada's youth also comes news of worrisome trends. The good news is that most of Canada's school-age children are doing better than they have in the past. More children are staying in school and enjoying access to computer technology. Crime rates among youth continue to decline, and employment rates for teens have increased. A connection exists between a modest level of part-time work and better school performance. However, increasing this level often has negative effects on school performance.

Worrisome trends related to technology and income are also occurring. A "digital divide" is taking place on the home front, with technology access related to family income. Widening gaps are occurring between Canadian youth enjoying school and community involvement with those who are at risk of falling behind economically and socially. Increased user fees for participation in quality recreation areas are creating barriers for equality in access. These recreational programs, such as art and music programs, swimming, and team sports, significantly contribute to optimal physical and emotional health.

Additionally, a divisive trend is developing in rural areas. These areas often receive inadequate funding for a variety of services. This seems especially to be true in funding for educational services of special-needs children.

The Prime Minister has stated that economic and social goals must be pursued hand in hand in the twenty-first century. He has spoken of the commitment of the Canadian government to establish an "investment timetable" to move toward the goal of ensuring opportunity for the youth of Canada. While some progress is being made and grassroots (local) involvements are striving to maintain and improve programs for all youth, much work remains to reverse the worrisome trends.

BEING "CANADIAN"

You have been reading about many elements of "Canadiana" in this chapter. So, what are common global perceptions of Canada's people? Tolerant, friendly, peace-loving, modest, and polite are descriptions one often hears.

Much of Canada's increasing population is a result of the migration of immigrants and refugees to the safer haven of Canada. Previous generations of immigrants welcome new generations of their families to Canada. The country is also becoming home to those fleeing oppression and persecution in volatile countries. This increasing population indicates the ongoing appreciation Canada has for its diverse population. Individual rights and freedoms are recognized under the federal legislation of the *Canadian Charter of Rights and Freedoms.*

Canadians do speak their minds and voice their opinions, but they do so with a polite openness to other ideas. Respecting differences and educating people about such differences are dedicated works of many individuals. Canada's regional distinctiveness offers examples of this "tradition of tolerance" approach as people across the country live their diverse lives.

REGIONAL DISTINCTIONS

The geographic locations of each of the distinctive regions of Canada are good descriptive tools to point out the differences in the people who live there.

Living in the North

Today, traditional activities mix with modern activities for people living in the territories of northern Canada. Children live in modern wood-framed houses, watch television, use the Internet, and attend school. Over the past decades, people have come to the North to work in the oil, gas, and mining industries. Usually, they work a short time for high wages, and then return to the more populated regions of the South, rather than settling in the territories.

Living in British Columbia

Mild winters and wonderfully scenic landscapes are key attractions for the nature-oriented residents of the highly populated lower mainland, coastal islands, and mountainous interior of British Columbia. A source of both beauty and wealth for the people, the forests of this region present conflict among the residents. Those who want to protect the original forests for future generations clash with the logging companies that log the forests for income. The fishing industry is also a source of conflict among the residents (Aboriginal vs. non-Aboriginal) of British Columbia, as are the "salmon wars" with the United States.

Living in Alberta

The oil and natural gas industries, along with agriculture, are important components of income for Albertans. In fact, they are the economic engines fueling much of the growth in Alberta, particularly in Edmonton and Calgary. Most Albertans live in cities and towns, but the ranching heritage of the past is still prevalent today. The famous Calgary Stampede offers ten days of rodeos, parades, and celebrations of cowboy ways of life.

Living in Saskatchewan

Saskatchewan has the highest percentage of Canada's population living on farms. Wheat, canola, barley, and rye are some of the main crops growing in the fertile flatlands of Saskatchewan. It is here that over 54 percent of Canada's wheat supply is grown. One-half of the province is covered by the boreal (northern, largely needleleaf) forest, which provides an additional important renewable natural resource for Saskatchewan. Located in the only province with entirely man-made boundaries, the capital city of Regina is home to the training academy for the RCMP.

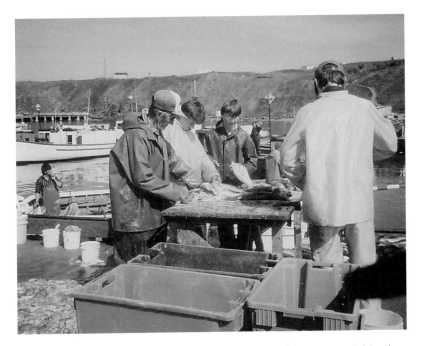

The salmon fishing industry once thrived in British Columbia. But fishing has fallen on hard times.

Living in Manitoba

Located at the center of Canada, Manitoba is an important transportation link between East and West. Major railways, highways, and airways pass through Manitoba. Winnipeg, Manitoba's capital, is home to more than one-half of the province's population. Although Manitoba has one of the lower population densities of the Canadian provinces, it is home to a number of large ethnic groups. One of the most important settlements of Ukrainian culture outside of Ukraine itself is centered in Manitoba. Significant Icelandic, Métis, and Mennonite populations further enrich the culture and economy of this province.

Living in Ontario

Most of Ontario's residents live in cities and work in the service or manufacturing industries. The automobile industry of the Golden Horseshoe region produces billions of dollars in exports of vehicles and automotive parts. Northern Ontario is a reverse image of the highly populated south. Here, small airplanes provide transportation for people and supplies from one forested location to another, as highways do not exist in this rugged landscape. The people living in Moosonee, on the southern tip of James Bay, do have the fortune of a rail link to southern Ontario!

Living in Québec

The culture and passion of French-speaking Québec has made Canada's largest province quite active on the political scene. Canada's largest hydroelectric power development in James Bay has also actively affected the people living there. Changing the courses of rivers and blasting high dams from solid rock have disrupted the lives of people and wildlife.

Living in the Atlantic Maritimes

Fishing, once the most important industry for this region, has fallen on hard times. As the people living here depend heavily on precious natural resources, any shift in resource supplies greatly affects the standard of living for the population. Oil has been discovered off the Grand Banks, but the high cost of extracting it has restricted its usefulness as an economic resource. Picturesque coastal towns and villages bordering the Atlantic Ocean have attracted millions of visitors to the Atlantic Maritimes. This has provided numerous job opportunities in the tourism industry for the friendly, welcoming people living in this region.

THE MOVEMENT OF PEOPLE, GOODS, AND IDEAS

Another aspect of geography is movement: how people, goods, and ideas move from location to location. Having just read about the distinct regions of Canada, you have been able to consider such patterns of movement. People and goods are moved via major highway systems and trains in the populated southern regions. Snowmobiles and dogsleds are used for movement of people and goods in the northern lands of provinces and territories. A well-developed network of commercial and for-hire air transportation—including planes equipped with pontoons for landing on water surfaces—helps move people and goods across Canada's vast distances.

The movement of ideas is a vision of *"Connecting Canadians."* This federal government plan hopes to make Canada the most Internet-connected country in the world. By becoming a world leader in the development and usage of the latest communications technologies, Canada stands to further benefit and empower its increasing population.

ENVIRONMENT

With or without an increasing population, a healthy environment is essential to a sound quality of life. Care for Canada's forests, grasslands, tundra, and wildlife are elements of this fragile balance. Air and water quality are also important in sustaining health and prosperity. The recognition of Canada's high life expectancy rate of 79 years is connected to the continued health of Canada's environment.

Combinations of federal and international initiatives are working to improve environmental concerns in Canada. Improved treatment of municipal wastewater, reductions in discharges of industrial pollutants and acid rain, and declines in fish and wildlife contaminants are goals on which Canadians are working daily to achieve.

LOOKING AHEAD

As Canada looks ahead, its shared border with the United States increases in significance for a variety of reasons. In the next chapter, you will read about trading issues, Canada's role in international development, and other vital issues as Canada moves into the future.

As Canada begins the twenty-first century, national goals continue to include developing technology to remain competitive in international markets; embracing immigrants, maintaining a multicultural flavor; and remaining a strong worldwide presence, both economically and politically.

8

Canada Looks Ahead

To more clearly see where Canada is going, it is beneficial to remember from where it has come. Its rich history commemorates, celebrates, and teaches valuable lessons not to be forgotten. Canada's identity has been shaped and ornamented by the contributions of diverse peoples. Referred to as a cultural mosaic, millions of Canadians live side by side, embracing their own and each others' cultures. Legacies of their diverse past continue in the existing traditions, beliefs, and values today.

BLESSINGS AND CHALLENGES

Canada welcomes its diverse immigrant population from many countries. There is an increased mobility of people worldwide. This has necessitated maximal planning for Canada as a destination for those seeking a better way of life. The success of a vigorous immigration program centers on two key factors: Benefits of immigration, such as economic growth and social enrichment, must be balanced with public confidence. This confidence is achieved through effective enforcement of immigration policies so that Canada's generosity will not be abused.

Nunavut's lesson, that aboriginal people can regain and govern their individual hopes and concerns, has offered a model of study for the world. Indigenous populations in Australia, New Zealand, and the Amazon region are discussing their respected places in society because of the self-governing status of Nunavut.

Historically, Canada's blessings of natural resources attracted explorers and investors. Nonrenewable resources such as oil and natural gas provide economic benefits for the country. Renewable resources, such as forests, are also capable of producing nourishment for the economy. Nurturing environmental management of all resources will be a responsibility for ensuring their preservation.

Major financial and social challenges face Canada's national health care system. Rising expenses and expectations, emerging needs, and new technologies contribute to pressures placed on the system. Reductions in federal financial contributions have forced the system to the limit of its ability to adjust. A health care crisis has arisen and urgently needs serious attention to maintain equal access for all—the desire of much of Canada's population.

Canada's desires in the twenty-first century integrate economic, environmental, and social considerations into its decision making. Capitalizing on technological successes will keep Canada competitive in the international marketplace. A knowledge-driven society is replacing the industrial-driven society of the past century or two. With Canada's innovations and developed technologies in use globally, one is never far from the spirit and pride that have made Canada what it is today.

CANADA'S INTERNATIONAL ROLES

Actively supporting human progress in developing countries is an effort Canada will continue to pursue. Assistance in the forms of knowledge and skill training, goods and services, and financial contributions have already occurred. By furthering social and economic progress of countries in transition, Canada advances its democratic and human goals of prosperity. Educated, healthy, and effectively governed people contribute to a world better tooled to solve problems. The establishment of stronger global economies will facilitate further growth and prosperity for these developing countries and, ultimately, for Canada.

The Canadian government will continue to work with its most important trading partner, the United States. Volleys of cannon and rifle shots have been replaced with volleys of words with regard to salmon, trade, clean water, and clean air. Significantly reducing smog-producing emissions is an environmental agreement that Canada and the United States are cooperatively trying to improve in the coming years. Maintaining secure and efficient access to each other's markets will be instrumental to the success of future trading initiatives.

Peacekeeping roles around the world are a proud record for Canadian forces. Strengthening democracy, justice, and social stability worldwide is Canada's vision of hope. The placement of men and women throughout the world who are daily pursuing this goal is a much-recognized worldview of Canadian strategy.

In the brief passage of time since becoming a confederation, Canada has risen to the rank of G-8 status. These eight most prosperous, privileged countries in the world are active policy makers in global trading and concerns. This G-8 status demonstrates the management of Canada's wealth of abundant resources and diverse intellectual capital of its people.

WHAT DOES THE FUTURE HOLD?

Canada is defined by more than its political boundaries or economic relationships. Knowing what brings Canada together, as well as what divides its people, is a vibrant process in Canadian identity. In the pursuit of this knowledge, one can see the tradition of tolerance that has respected the past and welcomes the future for Canada.

Facts at a Glance

Physical Geography

Area	3,851,814 square miles (9,976,140 square kilometers)
Coastline	151,485 miles (243,791 kilometers)
Climate	Varies from temperate in the South to subarctic and arctic in the North
Highest Point	Mount Logan, 19,551 feet (5,959 meters)
Natural Resources	Minerals, fish, timber, coal, petroleum, natural gas, hydropower
Land Use	Forests and woodland: 54 percent
	Arable land: 7 percent
	Other: 39 percent
Major Rivers	St. Lawrence, Mackenzie, Yukon, Fraser, Red
Provinces (10)	British Columbia, Alberta, Saskatchewan, Manitoba, Ontario, Québec, New Brunswick, Nova Scotia, Newfoundland, Prince Edward Island
Territories (3)	Yukon Territory, the Northwest Territories, Nunavut

People

Population	31 million
Population Density	8 people per square mile (3 people per square kilometer)
Population Distribution	Urban, 80 percent; rural, 20 percent
Life Expectancy	79 years
Literacy Rate	97 percent
Major Cities	Vancouver, Calgary, Toronto, Ottawa, Montréal, Québec City, Halifax
Capital	Ottawa
Official Languages	English and French
Religions	Roman Catholic, 46 percent; Protestant, 36 percent; other, 18 percent
National Anthem	"O Canada"

Government

Form of Government   Confederation with parliamentary democracy; Parliament consists of two houses: a 301-member House of Commons, whose members are elected by the people, and a 104-member Senate, whose members are appointed by recommendation of the Prime Minister

Head of Government   Prime Minister

Chief of State   British Crown, represented in Canada by the Governor General

Cabinet   Panel of ministers appointed by the Prime Minister from members of the majority party in Parliament

Voting Rights   All Canadian citizens over age 18 can vote

Independence   July 1, 1867, from the United Kingdom

Economy

Currency   Canadian dollar (CDN$)

Chief Exports   Wheat and other agricultural products, newsprint, wood pulp, lumber, petroleum, natural gas, metals, telecommunications equipment, motor vehicles and parts, manufactured goods, hydroelectricity

Major Economic Partners   United States, Japan, United Kingdom

Key Economic Sectors   Service sector, 67 percent of Canada's gross domestic product (GDP); industrial sector, 25 percent; agriculture, 2 percent

Per Capita Income $24,800 (US$)

25,000 B.C.	Earliest evidence of human presence in what is now Canada
1000 A.D.	Vikings establish a settlement at L'Anse aux Meadows in northern Newfoundland
1497	John Cabot reaches Canada's Atlantic coast
1534	Jacques Cartier explores Gulf of St. Lawrence
1547	Maps begin showing reference to land north of the St. Lawrence River as "Canada"
1608	Samuel de Champlain establishes the settlement of Québec on the St. Lawrence River
1610	Henry Hudson explores a bay that is later named for him, Hudson Bay
1670	The Hudson's Bay Company is founded
1754	Beginning of the French and Indian War in America, though not officially declared for another two years
1763	The Treaty of Paris forces France to surrender New France (French territory east of the Mississippi River) to Great Britain
1774	New France is placed under British North American rule as a result of the Québec Act; the act also guarantees religious freedom for Roman Catholics
1776	The American Revolution begins; Loyalists seek refuge in Canada
1791	The Constitutional Act of 1791 divides Québec into Upper Canada and Lower Canada
1793	Alexander Mackenzie crosses Canada to reach the Pacific coast
1812	Red River settlement established in Manitoba by Lord Selkirk
1812–1814	The War of 1812 is fought between the United States and Great Britain; U.S. attempts to occupy Canada fail
1841	The Act of Union unites Upper and Lower Canada into the Province of Canada
1867	Confederation—The British North American Act establishes the Dominion of Canada; Sir John A. Macdonald becomes the first Prime Minister

1869 Canada purchases Rupert's Land from the Hudson's Bay Company

1870 Louis Riel leads Métis resistance in the Red River uprising

1873 Royal Canadian Mounted Police (RCMP) are formed

1875 First public ice hockey exhibition played in Montréal

1885 Canada's transcontinental railway is completed

1897 The Klondike Gold Rush begins

1914–1918 More than 600,000 Canadians serve in the Allied forces during World War I; more than 60,000 die

1917 Income tax introduced as a temporary wartime measure, but remains in effect indefinitely

1929 The Great Depression begins

1939–1945 More than 1 million Canadians serve in World War II; almost 100,000 die

1945 Canada joins the United Nations

1949 Canada, the United States, and 10 western European countries form the North American Treaty Organization (NATO)

1950–1953 Canadian troops serve in the U.N. forces during the Korean War

1957 Lester B. Pearson, future Prime Minister, wins the Nobel Peace Prize for helping to resolve the Suez Crisis

1960 Aboriginal Peoples receive right to vote

1965 Canada adopts a new flag for the country, consisting of two red bands, separated by one white band with a red maple leaf in its center

1980 Québec's first referendum attempts and fails to obtain "sovereign association"

1981 Terry Fox dies of cancer, without being able to complete his cross-Canada Marathon of Hope

1982 The Constitution Act is passed, meaning Canada is now free to interpret and amend the constitution without referring to British Parliament (the "repatriation" or bringing home of the constitution)

1988 The 1988 Winter Olympics are held in Calgary, Alberta

1988 Canadian Multiculturalism Act affirms recognition and value of rich cultural diversity

1992 Toronto Blue Jays win baseball's World Series

1993 Toronto Blue Jays again win World Series

1993 Jean Chrétien becomes Prime Minister when the Liberal Party obtains the majority of seats in Parliament

1994 The North American Free Trade Agreement (NAFTA) takes effect between Canada, the United States, and Mexico

1995 Second referendum, and failure, by Québec to secede from Canada

1999 Nunavut officially named Canada's third territory and is self-governed by the Inuit living there

2001 Census records a population of approximately 31 million people in Canada

Barlas, Robert, and Norman Tompsett. *Canada.* Countries of the World. Milwaukee: Gareth Stevens Publishing, 1998.

Boraas, Tracey. *Canada.* Mankato, Minnesota: Bridgestone Books, 2002.

Bowers, Vivien. *Wow Canada!* Toronto: Owl Books, 1999.

Corriveau, Danielle. *The Inuit of Canada.* Minneapolis: Lerner Publications Company, 2002.

Grabowski, John F. *Canada.* Modern Nations of the World. San Diego: Lucent Books, 1998.

Kalman, Bobbie. *Canada the Culture; Canada the Land; Canada the People; Canada Celebrates Multiculturalism.* New York: Crabtree, 1993.

Odynak, Emily. *Early Canada.* Kanata, the Canadian Studies Series. Calgary: Weigl Educational Publishers, 1998.

Wallace, Mary. *The Inuksuk Book.* Toronto: Owl Books, 1999.

Internet Sites

http://atlas.gc.ca/site/english/index.html

www.cbc4kids.cbc.ca

www.communication.gc.ca/kclinks_e.html

www.connect.gc.ca

www.nlc-bnc.ca/kids/index-e.html

www.schoolnet.ca

www.thecanadianencyclopedia.com

Index

Picture Credits

About the Author

KRISTI DESAULNIERS enjoys incorporating her travel experiences with students' learning. As an elementary school teacher with a Master's Degree in geography, Ms. DeSaulniers has taught in England, Switzerland, and her home state of South Dakota. She also studied as a Keizai Koho Center Fellow in Japan. Recipient of a Distinguished Teaching Achievement Award from the National Council for Geographic Education, she has also taught in Canada on a Fulbright Exchange. Ms. Desaulniers currently resides in Sioux Falls, South Dakota, with her husband, Rob, in a home with memories, mementoes, and maps of travels.

CHARLES F. ("FRITZ") GRITZNER is Distinguished Professor of Geography at South Dakota University in Brookings. He is now in his fifth decade of college teaching and research. During his career, he has taught more than 60 different courses, spanning the fields of physical, cultural, and regional geography. In addition to his teaching, he enjoys writing, working with teachers, and sharing his love for geography with students. As consulting editor for the MODERN WORLD NATIONS series, he has a wonderful opportunity to combine each of these "hobbies." Fritz has served as both president and executive director of the National Council for Geographic Education and has received the Council's highest honor, the George J. Miller Award for Distinguished Service.